Mapping Connections

Indo-Thai

Historical and Cultural Linkages

Mapping Connections

Indo-Thai
Historical and Cultural Linkages

Edited by

Sachchidanand Sahai
Neeru Misra

MANTRA
BOOKS

First published in 2006, by Mantra Books, New Delhi.

This book has been made possible with support from the Royal Thai Embassy, New Delhi.

MANTRA BOOKS
C-401
Vimal Cooperative Group Housing
Plot No. 3 Sector XII, Dwarka
New Delhi – 110045

Distributed by Manohar Publishers & Distributors, 4753/23 Ansari Road, Daryaganj, New Delhi – 110002. Ph: 011-23289100/23284848.

Printed at Print Tech, New Delhi.

ISBN 81-902304-5-X

CONTENTS

Foreword
Indo-Thai Historical and Cultural Linkages

SACHCHIDANAND SAHAI
NEERU MISRA

The Royal Thai Embassy in cooperation with the Indian Council for Cultural Relations hosted a Seminar on Indo-Thai Historical and Cultural Linkages on 5 and 6 September 2005 at the India International Centre, New Delhi.

The proposed Seminar was visualized as an academic exercise preparatory to the establishment of a Thai Cultural Centre in New Delhi. The main objective of the Seminar was to analyze and outline the uniqueness of Thai culture and its contribution to the formation of a global Asian civilization as an equal partner with India for at least two thousand years of the recorded history.

Thailand is a sort of a bridge (not in a metaphorical, but in a real, physical sense) which links China, mainland Southeast Asia with Indonesia, Australia and Madagascar. In other words since time immemorial she connects the Indian Ocean with the Pacific and provides a cultural and commercial corridor for connecting peoples of distant lands. The importance of this geo-physical corridor became obvious at the time when the first India-ASEAN car rally was held recently.

The Seminar will project the role and image of Thailand as the custodian of all strands of Asian civilization, while watchfully preserving its own cultural identity. The pre-historic Bronze Age civilization of Ban Chiang in northeast Thailand requires closer attention from Indian and Thai archaeologists to outline the cultural exchanges of the distant past. The relics of the Dvaravati civilization of Mon origin around Nakhon Pathom and the Khmer civilization in the northeastern Thailand are carefully preserved by the Thai Fine Arts Department. The monuments inspired by the Sri Vijaya art of Indonesia in the southern part of Thailand are also an integral part of her cultural heritage.

These pan-Asian cultural components have been admirably synthesized and refined in Thai civilization whose foundations were laid in the valley of the Chao Phraya river in the 12th century under the leadership of the great Thai King Ramakamhaeng in the Sukhothai period followed by the consistent efforts of the kings of Ayuthya and the Chakri kings of Bangkok. The essence of this civilization has been a healthy and harmonious development of village and city (Baan-Muang) life, a problem which stares at humanity at the turn of the 21st century and its beliefs. Another Buddhist monk who has helped Thai intellectual community tremendously, to understand how to apply Buddhist principles for alternative development, is Phra Dhanuna Pitak or Bhikkhu Payutto, a Thai scholar of Theravada Buddhism. The Seminar, as expected, suggested practical ways to use Buddhism as the most effective component of Indo-Thai cultural relations.

Thai history shows how artificial our division of the past in ancient, medieval and modern is. Modern Thailand is distinguished by industrial and technological developments and by the refinement of its ancient traditions of dance, drama and music, inspired by the Theravada Buddhist traditions of the Jatakas and the Brahmanical tradition of the Ramayana (Ramakian). The Vessantara Jataka in modern Thai art and culture is a living example of Thai symbiosis of tradition and modernity. The Seminar focused on the dilemma of tradition and modernity while reexamining the historical linkages between India and Thailand. A closer look at the Ramayana/Ramakian certainly provided new insights to resolve the tensions between tradition and modernity faced not only by India and Thailand, but by the world at large.

The various phases of art in Thailand – the Dvaravati, Khmer, Sukhothai, Ayuthaya and Chakri – were taken into consideration. The art of Chiangrai and Chiangsen were of particular focus to bring out its relationship with the Pala art of India.

As was expected, the proposed Seminar provided new directions in linguistic studies, offering further clarities about the process of Indo-Thai cultural contacts. There is an obvious impact of Sanskrit, Pali and Prakrit on the Thai language. Thai vocabulary includes a large number of technical terms from these languages. Even in modern times the Thai resort to Sanskrit vocabulary to form new technical words which they require. *Thorasap* (*durasabda*), *Vithayu* (*vidyut*), *Akson* (*aksara*) designate respectively the telephone, the radio, and the alphabet. However, Thai and Sanskrit are languages of two different families. Thai is a tonal, non-inflectional language, while Sanskrit and the related languages of the Indo-Aryan family are polysyllabic, inflectional languages. So a Sanskrit word borrowed in Thai undergoes considerable transformation, both morphological and semantic. King Ramakhamhaeng of the Sukhothai period is the real founder of Indo-Thai linguistic cooperation. He invented the Thai alphabet based on the alphabet system of India. He had to add more consonant sounds for which there is no equivalent in the Indo-Aryan languages. In brief, the process of the Thai-ization of the Indic languages in Thailand, offers a whole new range of research possibilities on which the present Seminar lay focus.

We expect that from the deliberations of this Seminar have emerged a blueprint of our proposed Thai Cultural Centre which could mirror the unique cultural identity of Thailand the image of Thailand as the custodian of ASEAN cultural heritage; and her long-standing cultural partnership with India.

We also expect that the deliberations of the Seminar will be helpful in identifying the linkages in the field of religion, art-archaeology and language as essential components for building up a future programme of close cultural cooperation between India and Thailand.

We are well aware that Buddhism is one potential linkage from the past which is a continuing living force in the present day cultural dialogue between the people and governments of the two nations. It would be worthwhile to discuss the significance of new archaeological evidences, suggesting the historicity of the past Buddhist linkages and its potential for future joint efforts. In the 3rd century BC, during the reign of Ashoka, a Buddhist mission consisting of Sona and

Uttara went to the Land of Gold (Suvamabhumi). In the Thai collective memory, "the First City" –Nakhon Patholll or Nagara Prathama – still survives as the city founded by Ashokan missionaries, Sona and Uttara, some 60 kilometres almost west of Bangkok.

The archaeological finds from Ban Don Ta Phet in west central Thailand are quite remarkable as they provide the evidence for a cultural exchange that took place between India and Thailand in a distant past. The etched beads from Ban Don Ta Phet most closely match the Indian specimens from the Ganga valley between about 600 BC and AD 200. These archaeological finds, due to their antiquity, support the historicity of a Ashokan Buddhist linkage between India and Thailand and call for the renewal of these ties through more effective programmes of cultural exchange. Mahayana Buddhism was a forceful area of cultural linkage between India and Thailand from the 10th century. Recently discovered inscriptions from northeast Thailand and the monument of Phimai suggest an active role of the Buddhist centre of Nalanda in fostering this dialogue. The role of modern Indian and Thai institutions has to be defined in continuing this dialogue which is a part of our shared cultural heritage.

Successive generations of Thais have responded to the demand of their time and learnt to preserve their Buddhist heritage in the changed circumstances of the period. Consequently Buddhism flourishes today in Thailand as a living tradition that offers us a promising field of future study. With the process of modernization Thai Buddhist monks and Thai Buddhist laity have played a vital role as a catalyst of social change. Buddhadasa Bhikkhu from Thailand, considered to be Nagarjuna of our modern times, started to search for a new Buddhist way of life in 1934. His main aim was to go back to the source to define "real Buddhism" as all antidote for the "materialistic" way of life and superstitious historical and civilisational linkages. We are ever prepared to foster and revive these.

As a further step in strengthening our cultural and business ties we very proudly opened this Seminar on the Indo-Thai Historical and Cultural Linkages held on the 5th and 6th of September 2005 at the India International Centre, New Delhi.

Inaugural Address

SHRI RAJEEV SIKRI
SECRETARY (EAST), MINISTRY OF EXTERNAL AFFAIRS, INDIA

❖

Excellency, Ambassador of the Royal Thai Embassy, Mr. Chirasak Thanesnant, Professor Sachchidanand Sahai, Coordinator of the Seminar, DG, ICCR, and other distinguished delegates.

It is a great pleasure to be here among eminent cultural representatives from Thailand and India. I congratulate the organizers of this seminar on "Indo-Thai Historical and Cultural Linkages." Events like these provide valuable opportunities for interaction in the cultures and the arts which enable the coming together of our peoples. This in turn helps the business and industry of our countries and in the exchange of perspectives between Governments and industries.

The 21st century is defined by knowledge and human capital and this is what gives strength to our Asian identity. This century, therefore, could well be perceived as the century of Asia's pre-eminence. This view is supported by the brainpower of Asian scientists and engineers, the dynamism of our businessmen and industrialists, and our intellectual and human resource capital.

All of us, India, Thailand and ASEAN, belong to a region with many natural complementarities. Strong economic, cultural, historical and civilizational linkages strengthen our bonds. We are ever prepared to foster and revive these.

Thailand, a cradle of heritage and tradition, bridges the Southeast Asian regions. She connects, since time immemorial, the Indian Ocean with the Pacific and provides a cultural and commercial corridor to connect peoples of distant lands. The importance of this geo-physical passage became obvious at the time first India-ASEAN car rally held recently.

Among the various high-level delegations visiting Thailand was the recent visit by the Prime Minister of India in July 2004. To quote from Dr. Manmohan Singh's speech delivered at the Inaugural BIMST-EC Summit, "Thailand has played a pioneering role in bringing the BIMST-EC idea to fruition and we thank you for staying the course and for your leadership role. It is now our collective responsibility to carry it forward towards purposeful cooperation. In achieving the objectives of BIMST-EC, I would like to reaffirm India's firm political commitment to regional cooperation for mutual benefit and wholehearted support and cooperation with our BIMST-EC partners so that we succeed in our efforts to translate ideals into meaningful cooperation on the ground."

This Seminar will help to project the cultural role and image of Thailand as the custodian of all strands of Asian civilization. It has simultaneously maintained the indigenous vibrancy of its Thai cultural identity. Pan-Asian cultural components have been admirably synthesized and refined in Thai civilization whose foundations were laid in the valley of the Chao Phraya river in the 12th century under the leadership of the great Thai King Ramakhamhaeng in the Sukhothai period followed by the consistent efforts of the kings of Ayuthya and the Chakri kings of Bangkok.

We expect that from the deliberations of the Seminar will emerge a blueprint of our proposed Thai Cultural Centre which could mirror the unique cultural identity of Thailand, the image of Thailand as the custodian of ASEAN cultural heritage, and her long-standing cultural partnership with India.

This coming together may be an academic intervention of sorts but it will surely make us realize how deeply we are indebted to various Thai influences in our daily habits. Can we forget that for Indians Thailand today is the closest and one of the most-cherished holiday destinations? The savour and flavour of Thai food features prominently in most Indian weekend plans. The recently held Thai Week, and the crowds, especially the young, it drew at the happening Ansal Plaza in the heart of the capital, is evidence to this interest that Indians have begun to take in Thailand. This youthful generation will drive the future growth of the global economy. Our two countries should work towards strengthening our mutual synergies, so that we are strategically placed to derive maximum benefit from the emerging opportunities. The Thailand-India partnership should energize this process to move us closer to our shared goal of making this truly the Asian century.

Address

H.E. Mr. Chirasak Thanesnant
Ambassador of Thailand

❖

Your Excellency Mr. Rajeev Sikri, Your Excellency Mr. Rakesh Kumar, Distinguished speakers, Ladies and Gentlemen.

I am honoured to be among such a distinguished gathering, the first of a kind collaboration between the Royal Thai Embassy and Indian Council for Cultural Relations.

There is no doubt in anyone's mind how closely India is linked to Thailand in different aspects. Thailand had been influenced by India since the 3rd century BC when King Ashoka sent a group of Buddhist monks as missionaries to the area which was then called Suwannabhumi. From then onwards, Indian culture, whether it would be the languages, namely Sanskrit and Pali and the various traditions and beliefs, have been moulded into the Thai way of life.

Thailand established diplomatic relations with India in 1947. Our bilateral relations were not so close during the Cold War due to differences in worldview and perspective. However, what kept both our countries together were the long historical and cultural ties that bound us together. And that is the reason why this Seminar is focusing on the four main linkages, namely, Culture and Art, Religion, History, and Linguistics.

At present, I can say with full confidence that the bilateral relations between India and Thailand have never been better. India has been transforming rapidly since it liberalized its economy in the

1990s, opening up gateways of cooperation in many fields. With the signing of the Framework for Establishing a Free Trade Area between India and Thailand in 2003, the economic cooperation is in full force. It further creates an opportunity for both nations to have closer people-to-people contact through trade and investment.

Thailand is home to a large community of Indians who have successfully assimilated into the Thai society. You can be certain to find a number of prominent personalities of Indian origin in the government, business and the social sectors. Moreover, Thai nationals who have graduated from India and returned to Thailand, have become eminent scholars and academics and proven to be valuable assets to the Thai society, as you will be witnessing for yourself during this Seminar.

Before we proceed, I would like to inform you of the objectives of the Seminar. The Royal Thai Embassy initiated this Seminar to promote the understanding of cultural, historical, religious and linguistic linkages between India and Thailand. The outcome of the Seminar would be the first step towards the establishment of a Thai Cultural Centre in India, which I hope would become a reality in the not too distant future.

After the conclusion of the Seminar here in India, the Embassy plans to organize a similar kind of event in Thailand, which we hope would generate sufficient support and interest to make it an annual cultural event between the two countries. This initiative of "cultural diplomacy" would strengthen and promote people-to-people contact and carry on the heritage of both our peoples. I look forward to future cooperation with ICCR in this regard.

May I take this opportunity to thank Your Excellency Mr. Rakesh Kumar, Director General of the ICCR, Professor Sahai, Assistant Professor Director of the India Studies Centre, Thammasat University, without whose advice this Seminar would not have been possible. I would also like to thank Mr. Rajeev Sikri, Secretary, Ministry of External Affairs, for inaugurating the Seminar as well as all the speakers, the organizers and participants for making this Seminar meaningful.

I hope all of us would have a fruitful deliberation and gain more insight into our bilateral linkages.

New Delhi 5 September 2005

Thai Cultural History: Its Historical Link with India

SRISURANG POOLTHUPYA

❖

Introduction

Compared with Indian culture, Thai cultural history is quite recent. Not counting the Indus culture that is prehistory, Indo-Aryan culture began in 1500 BC, if not before. Thai cultural history, counting from the pre-Sukhothai (pre-Sukhodoya) period when the Thais still lived in small, separate city-states can only be traced back to about the 10th century AD. Before that, it is believed that there were Indianized cities or states in what was known as Suvarnabhumi or the Land of Gold. There are several Buddhist Jataka stories relating journeys of some Indians to Suvarnabhumi. There are also similar stories told in the Brihatkatha, a collection of stories, about voyages to Suvarnabhumi. As both collections of stories are dated before the Christian Era,[1] it means that the Thais, if they existed then, had cultural linkage with India more than 2000 years ago. Indian traders had made their presence in Takkola or modern Takua Pa which was their first landing stage.[2] They were also in Ligor which is now Nakhon Si Thammarat, Jaya (Chaiya), and Patalung (Phathalung), all in south Thailand. Therefore, it can be said

---

[1] R. C. Majumdar, *Hindu Colonies in the Far East* (Calcutta: Firma K. L. Mukhopadhyay, 1973), 9-10.

[2] R. C. Majumdar, *Ancient India* (Delhi: Motilal Banarsidass, 1974), 476.

that Indian cultural link with Thailand has begun before the Christian era and before the Thai Nation-State was formed. Thai cultural history can be divided into four periods as follows: the first period is called the pre-Sukhothai period, the second is the Sukhothai period, the third is the Ayutthaya period and the fourth is the Rattanakosin (Ratnakosindra) period when Bangkok or Krung Thep (Deva) is the capital of Thailand. The Thonburi period of only fifteen years is omitted.

The Pre-Sukhothai Period

We do not know exactly when the Thais came to live where Thailand is now. According to Prasert Na Nagara, the Thais "should settle here as a minority class for at least three or four hundred years before Sukhothai."[3] It means that the Thais have been here as early as 9th century AD. Some might live in small city-states while others were ruled by the Mons or Khmers who, at their zenith of power, held hegemony over the north, north-east and central areas that are now Thailand. The Mons of Dvaravati Kingdom on the Lower Menam (Chao Phraya river) valley might have established Nakhon Pathom (Nagara Pathama) as its capital.[4] It became a powerful kingdom in the 7th century AD. The Mons' power might have spread to North Siam and even West Laos.[5] Dvaravati flourished until the 10th century when the Khmers of Kambuja extended their supremacy over the Lower Menam valley.[6] The Khmers' power gradually spread to the north and other parts of Siam until the Thais overthrew them and established the Kingdom of Sukhothai.

During this pre-Sukhothai period, the Thais received Indian influence via the Mons and Khmers. The Thais might have already become Buddhist through getting in touch with China which accepted Buddhism in the Han Dynasty in the 1st century AD. However, most Thais believe in Theravada Buddhism which is different from the

---

[3] Prasert Na Nagara, *Some Topics on Old Siam* (Bangkok: Amarin Printing and Publishing, 1993), 51.

[4] Siriwat Kamwansa, *Indian Influence in Southeast Asia* (focusing on Thailand) (Bangkok: Akson Chareontat, 1979), 44. (In Thai).

[5] R. C. Majumdar, *Ancient India*, 484.

[6] R. C. Majumdar, *Hindu Colonies in the Far East*, 253.

Chinese belief. Kambuja also believed in Mahayana Buddhism. Therefore, the Thais might have received Theravada Buddhism from the Mons. The story of King Ashoka the Great sending two monks to propagate Buddhism in Suvarnabhumi, thus establishing the early and true form of Buddhism in this region, may help explain also why the Thais are Theravada Buddhists up to the present day. The Jataka stories also helped to instill Buddhism and Buddhist dharma in the people.

Thai people also received Hindu influence during this period from both the Mons and Khmers. Images of Hindu gods are found in archaeological sites all over Thailand. The belief in Hindu gods may be due to literary influence, especially the Indian epics Mahabharata and Ramayana. These sacred scriptures of Hinduism are open to people of all classes. The belief in reincarnation both in Buddhism and Hinduism led the Thais to literary creativity as well as the path of virtue. Some oral literary works existed in this period but were written down much later. For example, the Chamadevivamsa tells the origin of a city-state called Haribhunjai which was built by holy rishis and ruled by Queen Chamadevi. It became a city-state in the 12th century. The oral story of Chamadevivamsa was written down in Pali in the 15th century. It was an old belief that any work of importance should be written in Pali to stress its worth or seriousness.

The Sukhothai Period

Three city-states united their forces to overthrow the Khmer yoke in the 13th century and established the first kingdom of the Thais called the Kingdom of Sukhothai as Sukhothai was the capital. The first king was Sri Indraditya. The very name of the king indicates the Indian influence which might come via the Khmers who were Indianized before the Thais. King Ram Kamhaeng Maharaj, the 3rd king of Sukhothai, created a Thai identity by inventing the Thai script in AD 1283. The letters bear a slight resemble to some South Indian scripts. Perhaps they were adapted from the Khmer script which had been adapted from South Indian scripts.[7] However, the real great

---

[7] Rajapandityasthan, *King Ramkamhaeng Maharaj's Stone Inscription No. I* (Bangkok: the Royal Institute, 1993), 9.

invention was the addition of consonants, vowels and intonation marks to produce the exact sounds of Thai words. The tradition of making stone inscriptions started by King Ram Kamhaeng must have been a direct influence from India. Reading the Stone Inscription No. I of King Ramkamhaeng, we find that Thai words were widely used in this period. There were few Pali and Sanskrit words. However, towards the end of the Sukhothai period, more Pali and Sanskrit words gradually came into the Thai language. This might have been due to the growth of Buddhism in the reign of King Lithai who also composed an outstanding piece of literature, *Trai Bhumi Katha*. It relates the three worlds according to Buddhist cosmology. The content of this work reveals a strong influence of Indian cosmology which may come directly from India, not through the Mons and Khmers as in the pre-Sukhothai peirod. The Thai script invented by King Ram Kamhaeng has developed through time until its letters matched those of the Devanagari script of India. As a result, the Thai script can be used to transcribe Pali and Sanskrit words into the Thai language although we do not always pronounce these letters in the same way as the Indians do. Knowing the Thai script, an Indian can recognize the meanings of the written words borrowed from the Pali and Sanskrit languages.

The Ayutthaya Period

A new political centre was formed in Ayutthaya (Ayudhya) even before the fall of Sukhothai. The name of the capital means "unconquerable." Ironically, it was conquered by the Burmese twice and after the second defeat, the capital was moved to Thonburi (Dhanapuri) and then Bangkok. The Kingdom of Ayutthaya began in AD 1350 and was destroyed by the Burmese in 1767. During this period the Indian influence became more pronounced. There were two-way trades between India and Ayutthaya even after India became part of British empire. The economic links brought about strong cultural links. The Thai kings adapted Indian court ceremonies for their own use. The most important one was the Coronation Ceremony or Paramarajabhisek. This ceremony includes the ritual bath using sacred water from the various rivers in the kingdom. Brahmins conducted most parts of the ceremony. The belief in the avatara or reincarnation of the god led kings to be named Ramadhipati, Ramesvara, Narayana, to name a few. Indian literature came to be known to Thai people of Ayutthaya. It inspired literary works such as Vessantara Jataka, the Ramakian and many others. The Indian code of law especially the Manava Dharmashastra had some influence on the Thai Code of Law called Kot Montian Ban in Ayutthaya which was revised in the Rattanakosin period and renamed the Code of the Three Seals (Kot Mai Tra Sam Duang). It must be noted that the Thais did not accept the Varna system of India. Yet the king, called Phra Maha Kshatriya in Thai, was considered most sacred and the highest. Other classes were mobile. People could move to higher classes according to their ability in a number of cases. The social and culinary cultures of India also penetrated into Ayutthaya. The "pan" chewing, welcoming guests with pan, all kinds of curry, eating with hands were Indian influence. Even Thai dresses might be adapted from India. Ayutthaya women wore a sari-like cloth in the same way as the women in Maharashtra wear on the lower part of the body. Thai herbal medicine and Thai massage might also have come to Ayutthaya from India.[8] All these Indian influences were carried down right through the Rattanakosin period.

The Rattanakosin (Bangkok) Period

The original name of the capital of Thailand from AD 1782 onwards is Bangkok. However, the Indian influence made the Thais rename the city Krung Dev Mahanagara Amara Ratnakosindra. This is just the first part of the name which is much longer. This part, which means Indra's jewel, is used as the formal name of this period. One may notice the gap of fifteen years between the fall of Ayutthaya and the rise of Rattanakosin. This was the Thonburi period when the Thais were still fighting with the Burmese and did not have much time to promote culture. However, King Taksin of Thonburi composed

---

[8] Buddhadasa Bhikkhu, *India's Benevolence to Thailand* (Bangkok: India Studies Centre, 2504), 18.

a few episodes of the Ramakian which again indicates the continuous influence of Indian culture.

King Phra Buddha Yodfa Chulalok Maharaj or King Rama I tried to preserve Thai culture that flourished during the Ayutthaya period. He revived customs, ceremonies, laws, and literature that were current in Ayutthaya. Therefore, Indian cultural influence on the Thais remains the same or even plays a more important part in Thai society and culture.The Ramakian which is the recomposition of the Ramayana in Thai language has existed since the Ayutthaya period. The shadow play or Nang Yai as well as Khon play episodes from the Ramakian. Only fragments of the Ramakian remain in writing after the fall of Ayutthaya. King Rama I wished to preserve this valuable literary work as national treasure. He supervised the composition of the Ramakian from the beginning to the end of the story. So Rama I's Ramakian is more important than any subsequent Ramakian, firstly because it tells the complete story and secondly because the complete story is depicted as mural paintings on the gallery surrounding the Temple of the Emerald Buddha. The Thai people can learn the Ramakian from reading or looking at the mural paintings as well as seeing it performed as Nang Yai, Khon and many kinds of puppet shows. As Rama I's Ramakian was either recollected or recomposed for the purpose of having the complete story, some parts were found unsuitable for stage performances. King Rama II therefore composed another Ramakian especially for performing Khon. It then became a tradition for a king to compose the Ramakian. Thus Rama I's Ramakian inspired other compositions of the Ramakian by King Rama II, King Rama IV, King Rama V and King Rama VI. However, these later Ramakians only narrate important episodes. If we study the Ramakian we can detect cultural influences from the various parts of India: north, northeast and south in particular. It seems that Thai poets chose stories as told by Indians who might come from different parts of India as traders or Brahman priests to Bangkok. Then the most interesting stories were chosen by the poets. As a result, the Thai Ramakian resembles the Valmiki Ramayana only in the main theme while the details are different. Buddhist belief and Thai customs are also added. The sixth king of the Rattanakosin period started the tradition of calling the Thai kings of the Chakri dynasty Rama. Thus he himself is called Rama VI and the kings before him are posthumously named Rama I to Rama V.[9] King Rama VII did not like this idea. However, he was still called Rama VII and this tradition was carried on. Our present King is called Rama IX.

King Rama VI was equally interested in Indian literature and western literature. He composed many Ramakian episodes and kept the names and the story very close to the Valmiki Ramayana. For example, in Rama I's Ramakian, Vibhishana who is called Bibhek is a coward. In King Rama VI's Ramakian, he is Bibheshna and a brave warrior like in the Valmiki Ramayana. King Rama VI also translated Shakuntala and Savitri into Thai dramas. He also rewrote the story of Nala as a dance drama. He composed the story of the ten avataras of Narayana called Lilit Narai Sip Pang in Thai. He also composed a poetical drama called Madanabadha or the Legend of the Rose, using Indian scenes and Indian names. This drama also has an English version by him. Therefore, the cultural link to the reign of King Rama VI is very strong.

It is interesting to note that in spite of the growing Chinese and Western influence, the Indian influence remains quite strong in Thailand. One explanation may be found in a work by Sunthon Phu called Phra Aphai Mani composed in the early 19th century. This Thai epic in verse started off almost as a parody of the Ramakian. The hero Phra Aphai is abducted by an orgress whereas in the Ramakian Sita the heroine was abducted. The abduction leads Phra Aphai into many adventures. He meets Utsaren, the Prince of Lanka, who is a white man. Sunthon Phu wrote about an English pirate's ship much bigger than the Titanic:

> They embarked upon the many storied ship,
> With carts and cars for conveyance,
> Hundreds of camels, donkeys, horses, cattle
> And small pavilions to sit and relax.
> Flower and fruit trees lined the building edge,

---

[9] Phra Ong Chao Chulachakrabongs, *Chao Chiwit* (Bangkok: Aksonsamai, 1971), 572-73.

Looking lush and beautiful
Saffron, sandal tree, black plum, longan
Were grown as if on the mainland.
They walked and enjoyed looking at armsmen,
Workmen and sailors from Java.
The graceful Suwannamali
Led them to the big house under sandal trees.[10]

There were many wars involving white people which might have come from the historical fact that England conquered Lanka and a part of India. India remains important for the Thais whether free or under British rule.

King Chulalongkorn or Rama V visited India in 1872 during the British rule. Western appreciation of Indian culture may explain Thailand's close cultural links with India during the British period. King Rama VI's interest in India originated from the English translations of Indian works although the king knew Sanskrit.

Western knowledge is focused in science and technology while India offers spirituality which even Westerners are impressed with. Indians under the British rule felt the loss of their culture and were glad to find that Indian culture was well-preserved in Thailand. Rabindranath Tagore wrote a poem, "To Siam," that well expressed Indian feelings about Thai-Indian culture:

I come, a pilgrim, at the gate, O Siam,
to offer my verse to the endless glory of India
sheltered in thy home, away from her own deserted
shrine, to bathe in the living stream that flows in thy
heart, whose water descends from the snowy height
of a sacred time on which arose, from the deep of
my country's being, the Sun of Love and Righteousness.[11]

While the Thai go to India to study or to visit Buddhist places of

---

[10] Sunthon Phu, *Phra Aphai Mani* Part III (Bangkok: Office of the National Culture Commission 2004), 96-97.

[11] Karuna-Ruang Urai Kusalasai, trans. *Buddha as Seen by Three Illustrious Sons of India* (Bangkok: Sukhabhab Chai, 2001), 42.

pilgrimage, Indians came to Thailand for shelter during the hard time under the British rule and during the post-independent riots because of the partition. They become prosperous in Thailand and the good news brought more Indians to Thailand. The cultural link becomes two-way. Indians in Thailand accept some parts of Thai culture while Thai people appreciate Indian culture. There are some organizations frequented by both Thais and Indians such as the Hindu Samaj and the Thai-Bharat Cultural Lodge.

During Rabindranath Tagore's visit to Thailand, he was requested by a Thai scholar to send an Indian scholar to work to develop good understanding between India and Thailand. Tagore advised Swami Satyanandapuri to go to Bangkok. Swami Satyanandapuri set up the Dharmashram in 1932 which became the Thai-Bharat Cultural Lodge in 1940.[12] This Lodge has been promoting cultural links between India and Thailand ever since. Swami Satyanandapuri retold the Ramakian in very beautiful English prose.

In April 1993, the India Studies Centre was set up at the Thammasat University through the effort of His Excellency A. N. Ram, Ambassador of India to Thailand and the Indian Community in Thailand. The Centre was inaugurated by HE Narasimha Rao, Prime Minister of India on April 08, 1993. Soon after this a Sanskrit Centre was also established at Silpakorn University. Thus the studies of Indian culture and languages including Hindi were promoted in Thailand to perpetuate good understanding between India and Thailand.

Conclusion

India plays a big part in Thai cultural history. This may be due to so many factors. Among the important factors are the following: first, India is the birthplace of Buddhism which most Thais believe in. Second, India is the repository of great culture. It is the land of spirituality, grand epics and literature in general. Before the rise of the West, India was the centre for the arts, sciences and culture of the world. Third, India is situated near Thailand. It is easy to be in touch and the exchange of communications

---

[12] Thai-Bharat Cultural Lodge, *Mahatma Gandhi Memorial* (Bangkok: Mahachula, 1991), 120.

has existed even before the birth of Christ. In the age of globalization and internet this link will remain strong always.

Bibliography

Buddhadasa Bhikkhu. *India's Benevolence to Thailand*. Bangkok: India Studies Centre, 2504.

Karuna-Ruang Urai Kusalasai. trans. *Buddha as Seen by Three Illustrious Sons of India*. Bangkok: Sukhabhab Chai, 2001.

Prasert Na Nagara, *Some Topics on Old Siam*. Bangkok: Amarin Printing and Publishing, 1993.

Majumdar, R. C. *Ancient India*. Delhi: Motilal Banarsidass, 1974.

———. *Hindu Colonies in the Far East*. Calcutta: Firma K. L. Mukhopadhyay, 1973.

Rajapandityasthan, *King Ramkamhaeng Maharaj's Stone Inscription No. 1*. Bangkok: the Royal Institute, 1993.

Siriwat Kamwansa, *Indian Influence in Southeast Asia* (focusing on Thailand). Bangkok: Akson Chareontat, 1979.

Sunthon Phu. *Phra Aphai Mani* Part III. Bangkok: Officer of the National Culture Commisssion, 2004.

Thai-Bharat Cultural Lodge. *Mahatma Gandhi Memorial*. Bangkok: Mahachula, 1991.

Sanskrit and Pali in Thailand Based on Early Inscriptions

CHIRAPAT PRAPANDVIDYA

❖

Indian Contact with Southeast Asia

The region known collectively as Suvarnabhumi and Suvarnadvipa, roughly implied, in those days, Southeast Asia. "There are many references to sea-voyages between Indian ports and Suvarnabhumi or Suvarnadvipa, in old popular stories in the Sanskrit works based upon the lost Brhat-katha, as well as Buddhist Jatakas, Jain Samara-ichcha-katha and other works. The heroes of most of these stories are merchants and, in a few cases, princes, or chiefs in straitened circumstances, who want to acquire wealth by trade or other means. The Kathakosha relates the story of Nagadatta who went to Suvarnadvipa with five hundred ships in order to acquire wealth. The Buddhist works Milindapanha and Niddesa also refer to regular trading voyages to Suvarnabhumi" (Majumdar, 1963: 7). An attempt has been made to prove that the Indianization of Farther India, that is, Southeast Asia dates back at least to the Maurya Emperors (c. 3rd century BC). Coedes, however, is of a different opinion (1968: 16). According to him, neither archaeological and epigraphic documents nor foreign sources can be dated any further back than the Niddesa which dates at the latest to the very first centuries of the Christian Era. It enumerates a number of Sanskrit or Sanskritized places that may be identified with Farther India (1968: lo.cit.).

The earliest written document found in Thailand so far is probably the seal inscribed with the Brahmi script of the 1st century BCE, found at the archaeological site at Ban Khlong Thom, Kuan Lukpat, Krabi province. It reads "brahmadinasa" which seems to be in Prakrit meaning "belonging to Brahmadina." The inscriptions in Prakrit were popular from King Ashoka's times till the Gupta period. Since the seals were portable objects they might be carried by the owners to different destinations at a later date.

Inscriptions in Sanskrit in the Early Period

Bhavavarman, grandson of Sarvabhauma, the universal monarch, that is, of the king of Funan, was well known to be a Shaivite. He ruled Chenla, the Cambodian pre-Angorian kingdom which was constituted after gaining independence from the Chams, during the second half of the 6th century. The centre of the state can be located on the middle Mekong, in the region of Bassac (Coedes, 1968: 66).

His dominion must have extended as far as the Petchabun (Sanskrit: Vajrapurna), a Province in the northern part of central Thailand, as evident from the inscription bearing his name discovered in a forest near Ban (village) Wang Phai, Vichianpuri (Sanskrit: Vajrapuri) District, Petchbun Province. According to what remains in the inscription it seems that he was the grandson of a Cakravartin, that is, of the universal monarch, and the son of Prthivindravarman (CNPT vol. I 1986:141).

A few inscriptions which are almost stereotyped have been discovered in Ubonratchadhani (Sanskrit: Utpalarajadhani), Buriram (Sanskrit: Puriramya) and Khonkaen Provinces. They tell us that Citrasena is the grandson of Sarvabhauma, and that in spite of his being the youngest brother of Bhavavarman, has obtained the name after his coronation as Mahendravarman on account of his power and perfect characteristics (of a great man).

He is mentioned in the inscriptions to have erected Shivalingas and the bull, Nandi, as symbol of his conquest over the whole territory (ibid.1986:163,166). These inscriptions seem to be the earliest documents that record the presence in Thailand, of Shaivism. King Mahendravarman ruled Chenla from c. 600 CE to c. 616 CE (Coedes, 1986:69).

He is again mentioned in an inscription in Sanskrit found at Chong Sa Chaeng, Prachinburi Province, to have dug a reservoir named Shankara which undoubtedly was related to Shaivism.

The inscription of Wat Khao Noi Si Chomphu

The inscription was found at Wat Khao Noi Si Chomphu, Tambol Klong Nam Sai, Ampher Aranyaprathet, Prachinburi Province. It is the earliest dated inscription found in Thailand so far and the only inscription ever found in Thailand that begins with an invocation to Vishnu. It is quite obvious that it belongs to the Vaisnava sect. What can be gathered from the remaining words is that in the Saka year 559 (637 CE) a certain lord of Jyesthapura whose name is probably Iuvarakumara and who is described as a good servant probably of King Bhavavarman II has erected an image of Vishnu and some gifts were offered for perpetual worshipping of the image.

Then follows the part written in Khmer which gives the number of items and the names of slaves that were offered to the temple (from the rubbing belonging to the Department of Oriental Languages, Faculty of Archaeology, Silpakorn University).

The Khao Rang Inscription

It is one of the earliest inscriptions dating back to the 639 CE, second only to the inscription of Khao Noi. It was found at Khao Rang Mountain, in Prachinburi province. It begins with a verse in Sanskrit the rest is in Khmer language mentioning the gifts to a Buddhist vihara. It contains some Sanskrit or Pali loanwords, namely, vihara, sarvapinda, kalasa, pallavka (CNPT, vol. I, 1986: 37-38).

Subsequently, there are other important Sanskrit inscriptions, just to name a few – the Ban Phan Dung inscription, the Prasad Sdok Kak Thom inscription, the Prasad Phnomrung inscription, the Hin Khon inscription (see Prapandvidya 2004, Mumbai; Prapandvidya 2004, London).

Early Inscriptions in Pali

Early Inscriptions in Pali, judging from the script, generally belong to the 7th-8th century CE. In the main, their concentration is in central part of Thailand, the region where the Dvaravati kingdom was located. The most popular inscriptions are those written in the famous Pali verse which gives the essence of the Buddha's doctrine:

> *Ye dhammâ hetuppabhavâ tesaj hetuj tathâgato*
> *Tesañ ca yo nirodho evajvâdî mahâsamano.*

(CNPT, vol. I, 1986: 67, 74, 77, 80, 85, 88, 91, 94, 102, 108, 120-21, 134).

The verse occurs in Vinayapitaka, the Pali Canon on the Disciplines, where Assaji conveys the message of the Buddha to a mendicant, Paribajaka, named Sariputta who later on became the chief disciple of the Buddha.

There are other Pali inscriptions contain the extracts of important discourses of the Buddha from the Tipitaka, the Pali Canon as well (CNPT, vol. I, 1986: 58-62, 98, 105, 111, 117-18, 125; Prapandvidya, 2004, Paris).

Appearance of the Thais in Southeast Asia

The Thai entered the history of Southeast Asia in the 11th century when there is a mention of Syaj slaves or prisoners of war in the Cham inscription. In the 12th century the bas reliefs of Angkor Wat represent at the head the great procession of the southern gallery a group of warriors who wear the costume entirely different from that of the Khmers and whom two short inscription identify as Syaj. They were very probably Thai (Coedes: 190-91).

Inscriptions in Thai in the Sukhodaya Period

Inscription of King Ramkamhaeng

It is the first inscription in Thai ever created. It was inscribed in the reign of King Ramkhamhaeng, the Great, the third king of Sukhodaya Kingdom, who invented Thai script in 1283. It dates back to 1292 CE. The Sukhodaya Kingdom was established in the first half of 13th century. The following are the Sanskrit (S) and Pali (P) words found in the inscription transliterated in Roman script:

- Srindraditya from (S) Srindraditya: The name of the first king Sukhodaya Kingdom.
- Bol: (S and P); bala: army, military force.
- Ram(khamhaeng): A part of the name of the 3rd king of Sukhodaya.
- Sukhodai from sukha+udaya (S and P): The name of the first capital of Thailand. The variant forms of spelling are Sukkhodai and Sukkhodai.
- Tribur from (S) Tripura. Its meaning in Thai is the city surrounded by three walls. This may be due the influence of the Purana relating to the destruction by Shiva of the three invulnerable cities of three demons – Tarakaksa, Vidyunmali and Kamalaksa (Shiva-Purana: 802-50).
- Pakpatu probably from (S) Kapata meaning the door panel. This may be due to metathesis. The meaning is the door (compare: Pintu in Malay).
- Sradha from (S) Sraddha meaning religious faith, belief.
- Buddhasasana (P): Buddhism.
- Barnsa from (S) Varsa meaning a period of three months compulsory for a Buddhist monk to remain in a monastery without staying overnight elsewhere.
- Kathin from (S and P) Kathina meaning wooden frame, strap of pole for carrying burden. In Buddhism the word exclusively means the cloth presented to the monks for preparing a robe.
- Boribar from (S and P) Parivara: surrounding, retinue. In the inscription the word means the gifts accompanying the kathina cloth presented to the monks.
- Dana: gift (S and P).
- Nadd from (P) Natti and (S) Jnapti meaning promulgation.
- Arainik from (P) Arannika. In the inscription the word is the name of a monastery for forest-dwelling monks in Sukhodaya. A variant form of spelling is Arannik.

- Bad from (S) Vadya meaning music.
- Bin from (S and P) Vina meaning Indian lute.
- Bihar from (S and P) Vihara. In S, it means a park, pleasure garden whereas in P it means: i) An habitation for Buddhist mendicant, a hut, ii) place for convention of the bhikkhus, meeting place, iii) (later) a large building for housing bhikkhus, an organized monastery.
- Buddharub from (S and P) Buddharupa meaning image of the Buddha.
- Nissaiyamud from (P) Nissayamutta meaning a monk who does not have to be under the close watch of his teacher.
- Ther from (P) Thera meaning the monks who have been ordained for ten years and above.
- Sila (P): Precept
- Mahather from (P) Mahathra: A monk of great seniority.
- Savgharaj from (P) Savgharaja: Supreme Patriarch.
- Prajna from (S) Prajna meaning wise, learned.
- Pidoktrai from Pitaka (P) + Traya (S) meaning literally three baskets but the actual meaning is the Pali Canon.
- Gru from (S) guru and (P) Garu meaning teacher, spiritual teacher.
- Sridharmmaraja from (S) Sridharmmaraja name of a city in southern Thailand.
- Attharasa from (P) with (S) influence Attharasa: Name of a Buddha image. Literal meaning: eighteen.
- Plu possibly from (S) Tambula meaning betel leaf.
- Acana, a name of a Buddha image, from (S) Arcana meaning worshipping/reverence, or from Arcana meaning image.
- Saridbhovs from (S) Saridbhavga (sarit+bhavga) meaning in the inscription a dam.
- Prasad (S) Prasada or palace.
- Debada from (S and P) Devata meaning deity.
- Bali from (S) Bali meaning in the inscription to offer oblation.
- Saka, meaning in the inscription-era, from (S) Saka, name of a race.

- Hay from (S and P) Hayayana meaning disappearance, destruction. In the context of the inscription this word is used as a verb meaning to disappear.
- Mahadhadu from (P) Mahadhatu meaning great relic of the Buddha. In the context of the inscription it is a name of a monastery.
- Buja from (S and P) Puja meaning worship, respect.
- Tan from (S and P) Tala meaning palmyra tree.
- Urisajjanalai from (S) Urisajjanalaya meaning the celebrated abode of good people. A variant form of spelling is Srisajjanalai. In the context of the inscription it is a name of a city.
- Cedi from (P) Cetiya meaning tumulus, cairn.
- Dhadu from (P) Dhatu meaning the relic of the Buddha.
- Dharmm from (S) Dharmma meaning the law, religious activities.
- Ubasok from (S and P) Upasaka meaning male worshipper of Buddha as distinguished from the Bhiksu.
- Sthabok from (S) Sthapaka meaning the founder of a temple/ erector of an image.
- Uriradnadhadu from (S) Uriratnadhatu.
- Manavsilabatr, a famous stone slab erected by King Ramkhamhaeng. It is possibly from (S) Manahshilapatra. Manahshila in (S) means red arsenic.
- Sala from (S) Uala meaning a hall.
- Buddhasala from (S) Buddhashala meaning hall for the Buddha.
- Radnadhar from (S) Ratnadhara meaning the stream of gems. In the context of the inscription it is a name of a cave.
- Subarnnabhum, name of a city, from (S) Suvarnnabhumi.
- Bejaburi from (S) Vajrapuri name of a city.
- Kudi from (P) Kuti meaning residence for a monk.
- Than from (P with S) influence Thana meaning a place. In the context of the inscription it is used as a compound with a Thai word as *thin*-than meaning a settlement.
- Gru-acarya from (S) Guru or (P) Garu+ (S) Acarya meaning in the context of the inscription a highly venerated Buddhist monk.

- Rajaburi from (S and P) Rajapuri, name of a city.
- Samudra from (S) Samudra meaning an ocean, sea.
- Hovuabadi from (S) Hajsavati meaning in the context of the inscription the name of a city.

Observations

Both Sanskrit and Pali words were found in the inscription, some of which are a mixture of both languages. This reflects the earlier prevalent usage of Sanskrit words in Thai. As a result, the influence of Sanskrit words were still used for Buddhist terms in spite of the fact that in King Ramkhamhaeng's period the Sri Lankan form of Buddhism was accepted as the state religion. Sometimes Sanskrit and Pali words constitute a compound with a Thai word.

King Ramkhamhaeng invented few more characters in addition to the Sanskrit and Pali characters that were in use during the period. They are: *kh* (used only with Thai words and probably pronounced as Sanskrit *kh*), *d* (probably pronounced as the Sanskrit *d*), *d* (pronounced as the Sanskrit *d*), *b* (pronounced as Sanskrit *b*) and *s* (used only with Thai words and pronounced as Sanskrit *s*).

- Almost invariably, *t* and *t* are turned into Thai *d* pronounced as *d* in Sanskrit; *p* is turned into the Thai *b* pronounced as *b* in Sanskrit; *v* is turned into *b*. In the last instance, this may reflect the influence of the pronunciation from northeastern India, especially Bengal. In modern Thai *g* and *gh* of Sanskrit and Pali are pronounced as *kh*; *j* and *jh* as *ch*; *d* sometimes as *d* and sometimes as *th*; *dh* as *th*; *d* and *dh* as *th*; and *b* and *bh* as *ph*. How these 3rd and 4th sonant consonants of the five series were pronounced in Sukhodaya period is not certain.
- *œ s* and *s* are retained in writing but the exact pronunciation is not certain. There are also confusions in usage among them.
- Double consonants usually follow *r* preceded by a vowel. This is in accordance with the Panini Sutra: *aco rahabhyaj dve* Thus, *dharmma*, *varnna*, etc., are the optional form of *dharma*, *varna*, etc.
- There are confusions between short and long vowels as well.

- *A* is sometimes pronounced as short *o* in *police* and long *o* in *lone*, short *o* in *pot* and long *o* in *long*. This reflects the influence of northeastern Indian pronunciation.
- The final *a* seems to be dropped almost in all cases.
- Palatalization of *a* to *e* occurs when *a* is followed by a palatal consonant.
- It is the usual practice to use a noun in Sanskrit or Pali as a verb. The verb-form of Sanskrit and Pali is not used in Thai language.

Inscription of Vat Srichum (c. 1341-1367 CE)

This inscription is one of the most important inscriptions from the point of view of the historical development of Buddhism that involved Sukhodaya and Sri Lanka. It records the visit of a Thai monk who was formerly a prince to Sri Lanka through India. It is also very important from the point of view of political development. It gives details of how the Thai principalities freed themselves from the rule of Cambodia, possibly soon after the death of King Jayavarman VII (1181-c. 1218). The following are the Sanskrit and Pali words collected from the inscription (CSS: 61-79):

- Tathagata: (S and P) an epithet of the Buddha.
- Mahather: (P) a monk of great seniority.
- Mahiyavgana: (P) a name of an ancient stupa in Sri Lanka that housed the hair relic of the Buddha (Geiger, 2003: 5).
- Mahamunisrimahadontadhadu:(S) Mahamunisrimahadanta-dhatu or the great tooth relic of the Great Sage, i.e., the Buddha.
- Srisradharajaculamunisriraddnalovkadibmahasami or (S) Srisraddharajacudamaniuriratnalavkadvipamahasvami or the proper name of a monk from Sukhodaya who visited Sri Lanka in the 14th century CE, probably in the reign of King Parakramabahu IV (1302-1326) when Gampola and Dedigama were the capitals of Sri Lanka (Seneviratna, 1990: 22).
- Lovkadvib from Lavka (S and P) + dvipa (S) Sri Lanka.
- Dontadhadu from (P) Dantadhatu the left eye-tooth relic of the Buddha. The left eye-tooth relic was brought from Dantapura in

Kalivga, India, to Sri Lanka in the 9th year of the reign of King Sirimeghavanna who ruled at Anuradhapura from 362 CE. Originally it was worshipped mainly by Sri Lankan Mahayana Buddhists (Rahula, 1956: 86-87).

- Sugondhacedi from (P) Sugandhacetiya the building that housed the tooth relics of the Buddha in Sri Lanka during the visit to Sri Lanka by Srisradharajaculamunisriradd-nalovkadibmahasami.
- Sri+naunamthum: A Thai prince during early Sukhodaya period, grandfather of Srisradharajacula-munisriraddnalovkadibmahasami.
- Sevyaraja from Sevya (S)+raja (S and P) to enjoy kingship; to ascend the throne; to become king.
- Nagarasukkhodai from nagara+sukhodaya name of the first capital of Thai people.
- Nagarasrisejanalai from nagara+srisajjanalaya: name of a city.
- Pradistha from (S) Pratisthana meaning in the context of the inscription to erect; to construct.
- Sriraddnamahadhadu or (S) Sriratnamahadhatu in the context of the inscription, it mean a stupa to house the relic of the Buddha.
- Naihoradi from (S) Nairrti southwestern direction.
- Gun from (S and P) Guna or excellence.
- Bises from (P) Visesa special, extraordinary.
- Praman from (S) Pramana as (adj.) as.
- Bad from (S) Patra meaning in the context of the inscription bowl for collecting alms used by Buddhist monks.
- Bol from (S and P) Bala or army.
- Sahay (S and P) Sahaya close friend.
- Abhisek (P) Abhiseka meaning in the context of the inscription to anoint.
- Sri Indrabodindraditya from (S) Sri Indrapatindraditya name of the first king of Sukhodaya.
- Srisodharapura from (S) Sriyauodharapura, ancient capital of Cambodia.

- Sukharamahadevi. Name of a Khmer princess given in marriage to a Thai prince.
- Khan (S) Khadga +Jaisri = Jaya+Sri, the sword of authority conferred on a vassal ruler.
- Namakiar from (S) Namakirti meaning in the context of the inscription – name conferred by ancient Khmer king on vassal Thai ruler.
- Ramaraj. Name of the son of King Sri Indrabodindraditya, first king of Sukhodaya.
- Pran (S) Prajna wise, learned.
- Dharrm (S) Dharma Religious doctrine.
- Sriraddnadhadu (S) Sriratnadhatu relic of the Buddha.
- Srisajanalai a variant form of spelling of Srisajjanalaya.
- Dharmaraja. Name of the grandson of King Sri Indrabodindraditya.
- Bun (S) Punya merit.
- Paricna (S) Parijna knowledge.
- Cedi (P) Cetiya tumulus, cairn.
- Acarabarnadhibala (S) Acara+varna+adhipala one who protects morality and the men of various castes.
- Kasadtradhiraj (S) Ksatra+adhiraja the king who is above other kings.
- Sthit (S) Sthita standing.
- Srisejanalai a variant form of spelling of Srisajjanalaya.
- Gun (S and P) Guna in the context of the inscription, it sometimes means gratitude.
- Gru (S) Guru and (P) Garu teacher, spiritual teacher.
- Bunya (S) Punya merit.
- Danabindibad (P) Dana-pindapata gift and food collected from devotees by Buddhist monks in their morning round.
- Sila (P) Sila precept.
- Bhabana (S and P) Bhavana in the context of the inscription it means meditation.

- Vadd (S) Vrata religious vow.
- Paribadd (S) Parivrajya or (P) Patipatti practice.
- Sivhol (S) Sijhala (Sri Lanka).
- Des (P) Desana religious discourse or Desa country.
- Bhasa (P) Bhasa language.
- Biar (S) Virya perseverance.
- Byayam (S) Vyayama effort.
- Prarthana (S) in the context of the inscription it means to desire; to have a yearning for.
- Bodhisajbhar accumulated merits required for becoming a future Buddha.
- Buddhapradima (S) Buddhapratima Buddha image.
- Sasana (P) Sasana teaching, religion.
- Andoradhan (S) Antardhana in the context of the inscription it means to disappear.
- Khsanti (S) Ksanti tolerance.
- Maitri (S) Maitri friendship.
- Sadttv (S) Sattva being.
- Marryad (S) Maryada the bounds of morality, any fixed usage or established rule, propriety of conduct.
- Savvon (S and P) Sajvara control of senses.
- Bab (S and P) Papa sin.
- Ubadyay (S) Upadhyaya teacher, spiritual teacher.
- Mitrasahay (S) Mitrasahaya friend.
- Srimahabodhi (S) Srimahabodhi sacred Bodhi tree where the Buddha attained enlightenment. Its southern branch was brought from India to Anuradhapura, Sri Lanka, by King Ashoka's daughter (Rahula, 1956: 57-58).
- Adhisthan (S) Adhisthana meaning in the inscription resolve, resolution, determination (Edgerton:15).
- Sriramadebanagara a place name.
- Jambudvib (S) Jambudvipa India.

- Grahas(th) (S) Grhastha a householder.
- Rajasiha lion.
- Nagaraj serpent king.
- Dharrmaraja a variant form of spelling of Dharmaraja name of a king of Sukhodaya.
- Hari (S) Vishnu.
- Gun an Bises = Gunavisesa in the context of the inscription magical formula; incantation.
- Dhanusilp (S) Dhanushilpa archery.
- Sovsar (S and P) Sajsara transmigratory world.
- Dadd (S) Dasa and (P) Dasa ten.
- Rajakumarabatra = Rajakumarabhrtya.
- Sovsarabhob (S and P) Sajsara-bhava transmigratory world.
- Anitya-anat (S) Anitya-anatma impermanence, soullessness.
- Sarrdha (S) Sraddha religious faith.
- Krayadan = Kriya (S)+dana (S and P). Kriya means sacrifice and dana gift.
- Marakata (S) an emerald.
- Pradihara (S) Pratiharya miracle, extraordinary occurrence (Edgerton: 392).
- Ascarrya (S) Ascarya wonder, wonderstruck.
- Sakala (S and P) Sakala entire.
- Nalatadhadu (P) Nalatadhatu relic of the forehead bone.
- Givadhadu (P) Givadhatu the relic of collar bone of the Buddha. It is said to have been brought to install in the Mahiyavganacetiya by the thera named Sarabhu, thera Sariputta's disciple (Geiger: 5).
- Dakhina-akkhadhadu (P) Dakkhina-akkhathatu right collar bone relic of the Buddha.
- Sihol (P) Sihala Sri Lanka.
- Sumanakud (P) Sumanakuta name of a mountain where the Buddha impressed his footprint (Geiger, 2003: 8).

- Mavalikagonga = Mahawaeligavga a name of a river in Sri Lanka.
- Chabravsi (P) Chabbannaramsi ray with six colors.
- Maniraddna (S) Maniratna gem.
- Pad(dma)raga (S) Padmaraga ruby.
- Baidu(rya) (S) Vaidurya lapis lazuli.
- Prabal (S) Pravala coral.
- Raddna (S) Ratna gem.
- Mahasarrdha (S) Mahasraddha great religious faith.
- Bava(sa) = in the context of the inscription it means ordination. Probably (S and P) Upavasa a fast.
- Buddha-uddaj (S and P) Buddha-uttama Buddha the Highest One.
- Bineskram (S) Viniskramana renunciation.
- Raddnabhumi (S) Ratnabhumi a name of a place.
- Sriraddnamahadhadu = Sriratnamahadhatu great relic of the Buddha or a name of a place.
- Sarrbenudenan (S) Sarvajnatajnana omniscience.
- Bihara-avasa (S and P) monastery.
- Bicitra (S) Vicitra variegated, beautiful.
- Carita (S) Caritra good conduct, peculiar observance. In the context of the inscription, it seems to mean tradition or custom.
- Kudi (P) Kuti residence for a monk.
- Asrajbad (S) Asramapada hermitage, residence for a recluse.
- Uddaj (S and P) Uttama highest.
- Bises (P) Visesa special.
- Barrn = Varna in certain context, it means kind.
- Rakksa (S) Raksa to protect.
- Ubosadth (P) Uposatha 15th day of the lunar month.
- Bavarana (P) Pavarana Buddhist ceremony performed by monks at the termination of Vassa, the period of three month during rainy season, during which monks must remain in a monastery without staying overnight elsewhere.

- Ubaddthak (P) Upatthaka a servant.
- Mahatheranuthera (P) monks of great seniority and of less seniority.
- Bhiksusavgh (S) Bhiksusavgha the community of monks.
- Sala (P) hall.
- Mahacedi (P) Mahacetiya great tumulus, great cairn.
- Han (S) Hajsa goose.
- Hok (S) Vihaga bird.
- Sadtavv (S) a variant form of spelling of sadtva or being.
- Indranil (S) a kind of tree.
- Daradhan (S) Antardhana to disappear.
- Id (S) Istaka or (P) Itthaka a burnt brick, tile.
- Baribavarn (S) Paripurna complete.
- Kris (S) Krsna an incarnation of Vishnu.
- Adhissthan a variant form of spelling of Adhisthan.
- Bura = Purana or pura old or in the time of yore.
- Prakid. In the context of the inscription, it means to assemble, to put together. It is probably from (S) Pracita amassed, accumulated, covered, filled.
- Barrn (S) Varna color.
- Indranirmid (S) Indranirmita created by Indra.
- Majhimades (P) Majjhimadesa India.
- Badlibudtanagara (P) Pataliputtanagara name of a city in India, i.e. Pataliputra, the capital of the Mauryas.
- Anomanadi name of a river in India.
- Pradistha (S) Pratisthana to erect, to establish.
- Ram (S) Rama an incarnation of Vishnu.
- Narayadeb (S) Narayanadeva Vishnu.
- Cyud (S) Acyuta an epithet of Vishnu.
- Savsarabhob (S and P) Sajsara-bhava transmigratory world.
- Andola (S) Andolana swinging, oscillating (Monier-Williams: 44).
- Medtaiyo (P) Metteyya a future Buddha.

- Godtamo (P) Gotama the present Buddha.
- Gatha (P) verse.
- Mahanidan (P) Mahanidana name of a text.
- Jadi (S and P) Jati previous births of the Buddha.
- Sridhankada. It said in the inscription that on the bank of Anomanadi River in Badlibudnagar there is a Sriraddnamahadhadu named Sridhankada. What it may mean is a great stupa on the bank of Krishna River which was known from 3rd century BCE till 1344 CE as Sridhanyakataka (Raa: 39-40; Subrahmanyam: 35-37). At present, the name of the area is Amaravati in Guntur district, Andhra Padesh.
- Taruk (S) Taruska the Turks (Monier-Williams: 451). It is mentioned in the inscription that the Turks destroyed the Dhanyakataka stupa and took away gold decorating the stupa.
- Ganana (S and P) counting.
- Carammakhan = Cammakhandha piece of hide. It is described in the Mahavamsa that the Buddha spread a piece of hide on the ground where there will be Mahiyavganacetiya (Geiger, 2003: 4).
- Pradisthan (S) Pratisthana to erect, establish.
- Kesadhadu (P) Kesadhatu hair relic of the Buddha believed to be installed in Mahiyavganacetiya in Sri Lanka (Geiger, 2003: 5).
- Baribhogadhadu (P) Paribhogadhatu in the context of the inscription, it may refer to the precious throne used by the Buddha and left in Sri Lanka for the Nagas to worship (Geiger: 7-8).
- Mahiyavganamahacedi (P) Mahiyavganacetiya.
- Ballav (P) Pallavka part of a stupa = harmika.
- Burbadis (S) Purvadisa eastern quarter.
- Kailas (S) Kailasa name of a mountain where Shiva resides.
- Bunyasajbhara (S) Punyasambhara accumulated merits for becoming a future Buddha.
- Mahasamudra (S) an ocean.
- Rassami (S) Rasmi ray.
- Suvancedi (P) Svannacetiya golden tumulus, golden cairn.

- Givadhadu (P) Givadhatu neck bone relic of the Buddha that was installed in the Mahiyavganacetiya in, Sri Lanka.
- Kos (P) Kosa cavity, box vessel.
- Anjuli (S and P) Anjali folded hands in salutation.
- Buja (S and P) Puja in the context of the inscription it means to worship, to pay homage.
- Dandabadd probably (S) Dandavat like a falling stick. It is a form of paying great reverence to a holy man.
- Bencavga (S and P) Pancanga a form of paying homage to a holy man.
- Ubama (S and P) Upama simile.
- Sthan (S) Sthana place.
- Rajakumaramahasami an epithet of Srisradharajaculamuni-sriraddnalovkadibmahasami.
- Buddhavga (S and P) Buddhavkura one who is destined to be a Buddha.
- Sadhukar (S and P) Sadhukara uttering the word sadhu.
- (Kong) Cakra the wheel.
- Aditya (S) the sun.
- Mahakusol (P) Mahakusala great meritorious action.
- Prakot (S) Prakata common, vulgar, commonly known.
- Buddhasas (P) Buddhasasana doctrine of the Buddha or Buddhist religion.
- Aranik (P) Arannika monastery for the forest-dwelling monks.
- Dhaja (P) flag.
- Badak (P) Pataka a banner.
- Dib (P) Dipa lamp.
- Dhub (S and P) Dhupa joss-stick.
- Gndha (S and P) perfume.
- Mala (S and P) garland.
- Yas (P) Yasa fame.
- Boribar (S and P) Parivara.

- Savghather (P) Savghathera elders among the community of monks.
- Dhudavg (P) Dhutavga a kind of Buddhist vow followed by a monk.
- Amatya (S) minister of a king.
- Rajasena Royal army.
- Ubasok (S and P) Upasaka male worshipper of the Buddha as distinguished from the Bhiksu.
- Ubasika (S and P) Upasika female worshipper of the Buddha as distinguished from the Bhiksu.
- Samadhi (S and P) meditation.

Observations

1. The development of orthography is noticeable when compared with the first Thai inscription of King Ramkhamhaeng. For in stance, *r* preceded by *a* and followed by a consonant is doubled and the consonant following the *r* is no longer doubled. This practice is a standard till today.
2. It seems that there is no distinction in pronunciation of the three sibilants.
3. The use of Sanskrit words is more prevalent than Pali. This may reflect the influence of Mayana Buddhism. During the time when Mahasrisraddharajaculamuni visited Sri Lanka the Mahayan Buddhism was prevalent there as well. Mahasrisraddharaja-culamuni's inclination toward the Mahayana faith can be seen from his resolution to become one of the future Buddhas.
4. There was confusion in the use of *n* and *n*. This reflects the non-distinction in their pronunciation.

Conclusion

Since the Thai entered the history of Southeast Asia not later than the 11th century, they must have absorbed Sanskrit and Pali vocabulary into their own language from then if not before through their contact with Khmers who were the dominant power in the eastern part of

Thailand and through the Mons of Dvaravati kingdom in its central part. We come to know for the first time how Sanskrit and Pali words appear in Thai language when the first inscription in Thai language was created in 1292 CE in the Sukhodaya period. In spite of the fact that the Sri Lankan form of Buddhism was accepted to replace Mahayana Buddhism which was dominant at that time the use of Sanskrit words is more predominant than Pali as can be seen from the two inscriptions in Thai languages studied in this paper. This suggests that the culture that had Sanskrit as its vehicle was deep-rooted in the mind of the Thai before the Sukhodaya period.

Bibliography

Apte, Vaman Shivam 1998. *The Practical Sanskrit-English Dictionary*. Kyoto: Risen Book Company.

Charuek Samay Sukhoday (CSS) 1983). Bangkok: Fine Art Department, BE2526.

Charuek Nai Pradeœ Thai (CNPT) Vol.I. 1986. Bangkok: Fine Art Department, BE2529.

Basham, A.L. 1982. *The Wonder that was India*. Delhi: Fontana Books is association with Rupa & Co.

Coedes, G. 1968. *The Indinized States of Southeast Asia*, edited by Walter F. Vella, translated by Susan Brown Cowing. Honolulu: An East-West Center Book, the University Press of Hawaii.

Edgerton, Franklin, 1972. *Buddhist Hybrid Sanskrit, Grammar and Dictionary*, Volume II. Dehli: Motilalbanarsidass.

Geiger, Wilhelm, trans. 2003. *The Mahavajsa or the Great Chronicle of Ceylon*. Dehiwela Sri Lanka: Buddhist Cultural Centre.

Majumdar, R. C. 1963. *Ancient Indian Colonization in South-East Asia*. Baroda: Oriental Institute.

Monier-Williams, Monier 1964. *A Sanskrit-English Dictionary*. Oxford: University Press.

Pou, Sevaros 1992. *Dictionaire Vieux Khmer-Francais-Anglais*. Paris: Centre De Documentation et de Recherche sur la Civilisation Khmère.

Prapandvidya, Chirapat, 2004, Mumbai. *Buddhism In the Eastern and Northeastern Parts of Thailand from 7th to 13th Centuries Based on Inscriptions and Archaeological Evidence*, a paper presented at the International Conference on "Contribution of Buddhism to the World Culture" organized by Somaiyya Center for Buddhist Studies, Mumbai, India, from March 10 to 16, 2004.

———. 2004, Paris. *Early Inscriptions Presuppose a Culturally Developed Society in the Proto-historic Central Thailand*, a paper presented at Euroseas Conference, Paris, September 1-4, 2004.

———. 2004, London. *Shaivism in Thailand as Recorded in Inscriptions and Old Documents from Sixth Century to Early Ayudhya Period*, a paper presented at the 10th International Conference of the European Association of Southeast Asian Archaeologists, EurASEAA10, London, from September 14 to 17, 2004.

Rahula, Walpola 1956. *History of Buddhism in Ceylon: The Anuradhapura Period, 3rd Century BC-10th Century A.C.* Colombo: M.D. Gunasena & Co. Ltd.

Rao, Hanumantha B. S. L. and others 1998. *Buddhist Inscriptions of Andhradesa*. Secondarabad: Ananda Buddha Vihara Trust.

Rhys Davids, T. W. and Stede William, ed. 1972. *The Pali Text Society's Pali-English Dictionary*. London: The Pali Text Society.

Seneviratna, Anuradha 1990. *Buddhist Rituals and Ceremonies*. Colombo: Department of Cultural Affairs, Government of Sri Lanka.

Sircar, Dines Chandra, ed. 1965. *Select Inscriptions Bearing on Indian History and Civilization, Vol.I.* Calcutta: University of Calcutta.

The Shiva-Purana, Part II, translated by A Board of Scholars 1994. Delhi: Motilal Banarsidass.

Subrahmanyam, B. 1999. *Buddhist Relic Caskets in Andhradesa*. Secunderabad: Ananda Buddha Vihara Trust.

Sanskrit and Pali
The Common Heritage and the Linking Bridge Between India and Thailand

SOMBAT MANGMEESUKHSIRI

❖

Introduction

Sanskrit is the most important language that moulded Indian life and thought in ancient, medieval, and modern times (until very recently). Sanskrit has also constituted the greatest literary heritage of the country. Without a knowledge and appreciation of Sanskrit, no knowledge and appreciation of Indian literature, such as the Upanishads, the Ramayana, the Mahabharata and the Puranas are possible. In the same manner, Pali the language of Buddhism, gets even less importance in its place of origin, India, but occupies the most popular place in Thai history, Thai culture and the Thai way of life from the Sukhothai (Sukhodaya) period till the present. Without the knowledge of Pali, Hinayana Buddhism cannot be completely known, and without the knowledge of Buddhism, the study of the Thai way of life is next to impossible.

Therefore, the purposes of this paper are: (i) to illustrate the importance of Sanskrit and Pali in the Thai way of life in modern times, that is how the Thais adopt Sanskrit and Pali in their daily life, and (ii) to show how they share this common heritage with the place of origin, India.

The Distant Past to the Present: Indo-Thai Relation Through Sanskrit and Pali

India and Thailand (the Indo-China peninsular or Suvannabhumi in the distant past) have been linked for some centuries before the Christian era, by traders and missionaries, especially the group of Buddhist monks led by Sona and Uttara in the reign of King Ashoka in the 3rd century BC. Subsequently, the relation between two subcontinents has grown immensely through the religious channels, that is Buddhism and Brahmanism. Simultaneously, Sanskrit as the religious language of Brahmanism and Mahayana Buddhism and Pali (or Magadh) as the canonical language of Theravada or Hinayana Buddhism were introduced from Bharata Varsha to Suvannabhumi. From that period till the present day, Sanskrit and Pali have not only brought literary heritage, but they also have picked up the way of life, the rituals, the way of thinking from India to Thailand. The Thai people always use Sanskrit and Pali words, either consciously or unconsciously, and Thai-ize both languages as their own heritage. For instance, in the Thai national anthem, the first word which is used is in Sanskrit. That word, *Prathet* or *Pradesh* is Sanskrit in origin. There are more than fifty per cent Sanskrit and Pali loan words in the modern Thai language.

Sanskrit and Pali in the Thai Way of Life: Naming People

The Thai language is very rich in words which we can use at our will. The Thai people owe this to Sanskrit and Pali, because when they adopted Sanskrit and Pali into their language, it made the Thai language contain more words and vocabulary than earlier. Sanskrit and Pali loan words can be readily used for many purposes such as communication in daily life, composition of verses and the most important, in the modern Thai society today, the naming of people.

During the reign of King Rama VI of the Cakri dynasty or the Bangkok period (1912-1925 A.D) the Thai were forced by royal decree to have their own surnames. Before this time, the Thai only had names and all of these were derived from the original Thai language. For example, Nai Dang (Mr. Dang or Mr. Red in English), Amdang Kham

(Ms. Kham or Ms. Gold in English), or from Khmer or Cambodian loan words, such as, Nai Amnat (Mr. Power in English). Naming people with Thai and Khmer original words was in use for sometime. But, a little more than sixty years ago, after World War II, naming people with Sanskrit and Pali words has been gathering popularity among the Thais. The reason why Sanskrit and Pali are very popular for names of people is because both the languages have many syllables, that is they are polysyllabic, unlike original Thai words which are mostly monosyllabic. Besides, the meanings of Sanskrit and Pali loan words in the Thai language are quite unique and sacred because both the languages are regarded as religious languages in Thai society. From then on till the present day, Sanskrit and Pali have played the most important role in naming the Thai.

Nowadays, however, the Thai have less knowledge of Sanskrit and Pali than in the past, when compared to our grandparents. But, even so, when people want to name newborn babies or desire to change their own unpleasant or unlucky names to auspicious ones, they always resort to Sanskrit and Pali. This is not only the belief or superstition of the older generations, but it is also the most popular trend among the new generations, even under the impact of western civilization especially the western languages such as English and French. It is quite an amazing fact that Thailand's new generation prefers English and French nicknames to Thai ones, and yet they never use these western languages for their "real" names instead of Sanskrit and Pali. Thus, we can safely say that naming people is the most important role that Sanskrit and Pali play in modern Thai society.

The Table below shows instances of Thai names of Sanskrit and Pali origin.

Thai	**Sanskrit**	**Pali**	**Meaning in Thai Concept**
Sombat	Sampatti	Sampatti	Wealth, posperity
Abhijay	Abhijaya	Abhijaya	Great Victory
Vichian	Vajra	Vajira	Diamond
Anuja	Anuja	Anuja	Younger brother
Kanda	Kanta	Kanta	Beloved girl
Janathip	Janadhipa	Janadhipa	Big boss, King

Anong	Ananga	Ananaga	Pretty (for women only)
Nakorn	Nagara	Nagara	City, Town
Sasikarn	Sasikanta	Sasikanta	Lovely like the moon
Netchanok	Netra Janaka	Nayana-janaka	Father's eyes
Suthee	Sudh	Sudh	Intelligent

Sanskrit and Pali in Coining New Words

It is worth noting that the contribution of Sanskrit and Pali towards the Thai language is unique and unparalleled, especially in coining new words and technical terms which came from other cultures, especially from the West.

"To coin a word is to put it in circulation with a stamp of authority – State Authority in the case of legal terms in the codes or laws or terms determined by the Royal Institute…"[1] "The rhythm of the word coined must conform to that required by the genius of the language." The above mentioned suggestion was made by Prince Wan Waithayakorn, who had also been the Chairperson of the Word Coining Committee and very famous in coining new words for use in Thai society. He also showed the easy way to coin new words, the only two principles which the Royal Institute is utilizing till date. The two are as follows:

- To create a new word: When coining new words, we must use the Thai word first. If we do not find any suitable Thai words which can convey its meaning well, both morphological and semantic, then we can coin a new word by using Sanskrit and Pali or combining them together to get a very close form and meaning of that western word.
- Transliteration with minor change: In case we do not find any Thai, Sanskrit or Pali word which is suitable to its English equivalent, we can use the word in its Thai original.

Instances of coining new words using Sanskrit and Pali words are shown in this table.

[1] "Coining Thai Words" by Prince Wan Waithayakorn. *Siam Society Journal*, in the Memoriam Phya Anuman Rajadhon. Bangkok, 1970: 33-38.

Western Word	New-coined Word in Thai
Seminar	Sammanaa (sam + manas)
Culture	vattanatham (vaddhana + dharma)
State	sthaana (stha + na)
Self Identity	Attalak (atta + laksana)
Video	veedithad (v-ti + darsana)
Multivision	Anekathad (aneka + darsna)
History	Pravadsaat (pravatti+sastra)
Logic	Takkavithayaa (tarka + vidya´)
Philosophy	Pradyaa, pradchayaa (pra +jna)
Galaxy	Daaraacak (tara+cakra)
Ultimate reality	Antimasad (antima + sacca)

To coin a new word is both a science and an art. It is very difficult to have new words just as we wish. Sometime it takes a lot of time to find even one word. Furthermore, we cannot expect that people will accept new coinages. In this regard, Prince Wan added another suggestion while referring to Shri Jawaharlal Nehru: "Suggestions have, therefore, been made that I should do a dictionary coining words as I go along, but I have refused because that is not the correct method. Raghu Vira has made an English-Hindi Dictionary, but even the late Jawaharlal Nehru admitted that the new coinages could not be expected to be used all at once. Indeed, coining words cannot be done at the will of the coiner; the coinage must have not only the meaning required but must lend itself to uses required in various contexts and must have a form acceptable to the genius of the language." This also has shown us the close relation between Thai and Indian illustrious scholars in coining new word by sharing our common heritage, that is Sanskrit and Pali.

To conclude this paper, Sanskrit and Pali are the most important heritages that Thailand has received from India. Why? Because Sanskrit and Pali are concrete bridges linking India and Thailand. In daily life, we think, we act, we speak under the influence of Sanskrit and Pali. Even now, English has occupied global communities, but the Thai society prefers to share this common heritage with India. Thus, to understand better both Indian history and culture and that of

Thailand, both counterparts must utilize Sanskrit and Pali as the common heritage to keep bilateral relations in the present and to further the cooperation in the future and lead our countries to prosperity and happiness.

Art Objects and Architectures Reflecting Indo-Thai Cultural Linkages

AMARA SRISUCHAT

❖

The aim of the paper is to pinpoint the phenomena of Indo-Thai cultural linkage by means of archaeological research on art objects and architectural remains found in India and in Thailand which are the evidence that serve to tell us over a long period of time of the socio-cultural linkages of the two lands. The following points are the result of the research on the matter:

1. Art objects and architectural remains found in archaeological sites of Thailand and India reflect the exchange of trans-oceanic trades between the two territories and the world-trade networks since the 4th c. BC:

It is evident that before trans-oceanic trades local people in Thai territory made a voyage in Southeast Asian region by boat. This is exemplified by a terracotta piece depicting two people on boat found at the Ban Chiang archaeological site (4th c. BC), Udonthani Province, Northeast Thailand. It is also evident that in the 4th century BC the Indian merchants came to seek mineral ores like tin and lead from Thai soil to make high-tin and bronze utensils and implements. It is indisputable that Thailand is a place for mineral resources like tin ore, lead ore and copper ore. At the Ban Don Ta Phet site, Kanchanaburi Province, Central Thailand, from where the high-tin bronze utensils were originally made, a leaping lion pendent and carnelian beads (from India in the 3rd to 4th century BC) were found; it would seem possible that the high-tin cast bronze vessels were imported to India from Thailand. This leaping lion pendant and carnelian beads found in the site suggest that these were the objects which the Indian merchant brought with them and they were buried as grave goods (prestige goods) in Thai soil.

In the early historic period, Indian coins depicting a stylized double-masted ship, found at the Khlong Thom site, Krabi Province, East coast of South Thailand, 1st-2nd c. AD, reflects the exchange of trans-oceanic trades between the two territories. During that period, etched beads which appeared in the Ganga Valley, India, between 600 BC and 200 AD, were found at two important port sites of Southern coasts of the Thai soil; Khlong Thom, the western port and Khao Sam Kaeo, Chumphon Province, the eastern port. It is conjectured that the stone and glass bead making and gold ornament making were introduced by Indian craftsmen to Thailand in the 1st century BC to the 3rd century AD. This is evident from a touch stone of a goldsmith with Tamil inscription. The text reads "Perumpadankal" meaning "stone of (Mr.) Perumpadan (Big Feet)," dating the 3rd century. This object was found at the Khlong Thom site. The readymade materials, i.e. beads and ornaments made of stone, glass and gold were sold again at other markets. On the other hand, new products like lead and tin bi-polar beads, manufactured for export, resulted from the introduction of technology from India and its combination with indigenous knowledge on metallurgy and the concept of art. The product had special characteristics and was even different from the product which it was modeled on. Thus the type of bead was in demand by markets including India. It is evident that this kind of bead was found at Virampattanam site in India. So that the cultural exchange of people from two lands through trade was developed into the world-trade network.

Commercial relationship between people in Thailand and India had developed into a political state affair in the medieval period. In the 16th century, the King of Ayutthaya, the sovereign king over Thailand, appointed a foreigner (to be a consul) to take charge of the trade station overseas, including India. One of the Muslim consuls was called Datoh Mugul, believed to be a man in the Mughal Dynasty (the Mughal ruled India from the 16th to the 18th century). Datoh Mugul was then appointed by the king to be a ruler of Singhora (the present Songkhla), the important sea-port of Southern Thailand. He made commercial transactions with European countries. He constructed town walls and fortification after European models. The remains of the ancient fortification constructed in the town remind us of the European fort at Goa on the west coast of India.

2. The discovery of significant images of Buddha in Thailand reveals the history of the propagation of Buddhism in early times:

Four bronze images of the Buddha were identified in the Amaravati style of South India and in the Gupta style of Sarnath, India. The two Amaravati style images were identified with the 4th-5th century images of Buddha from the Nakhon Ratchasima Province, Northeast Thailand, and from Sungai Golok, Narathiwat Province, South Thailand. The latter has the drapery characteristic of the image fitting in with those of the Buddhist monk of the Mahasanghika sect described in the records of the Chinese monk who visited India. It is conjectured that the Mahasanghika sect was initially introduced to Thailand. The two bronze images of Buddha which were identified in the Gupta style from Sarnath, India, are from the Wiang Sa, Suratthani Province, Southern Thailand and from the Phong Tuk, Kanchanaburi Province, Central Thailand, dating back to the 5th century to the 7th century.

3. The concordance between indigenous belief and Hindu belief:

The acceptance of indigenous people on Thai soil of the worship of the Shiva Linga (the divine phallic symbol) of Hinduism from India resulted from the intermingling with the indigenous belief in phallus worship for fertility rites of the early agricultural community in Thailand since 1000 BC. It is evident that terracotta in the form of male and female genitals was found at the 1st century port sites like Khao Sam Kaeo, Chumphon Province. Not far from the site, a Mukhalinga of the 8th-9th century was found at the Nong Wai site, Thachana District, Suratthani Province. The Mukhalinga is a linga with the face of Shiva (a Hindu God) in human form in the middle of the linga, showing His Supreme power according to the myth in the Puranas. The linga of Nong Wai is comparable to that of the 5th century Gupta art of India. The widespread tradition of making and worshipping Shiva Lingas all over Thailand took place between the 6th c. and the 9th c. AD. The art of making it followed Indian philosophy and myths. So that most Shiva Lingas found in Thailand are similar to those found in India. In later periods there are also sculptures showing the presence of Shiva in human form in Thailand, but they were made after the 10th c. AD. In this aspect, Shiva is naked showing his genital. An interesting representation of the Shiva in human form is the Bhairava. The mid-11th century Shiva as the Bhiksatana from Tiruvenkadu, Tamil Nadu and the 15th century Bhairava from South India are comparable to the 11th century Bhairava found at Wiang Sa, Suratthani, Southern Thailand. This depicts the influence of Chola art in Southern Thailand at that time.

4. The harmonization of two main religious beliefs from India in Thai territory:

The acceptance of the role of Hinduism in the Buddhist community was exemplified by Buddhist sculptures of the 7th to 8th century of Dvaravati communities that depicted Lord Buddha as the principal of the scene and provided a proper space for the figures of the Hindu gods or of the Yogi. For instance the presence of Shiva and Vishnu in the scene of Lord Buddha preaching Dharma on the wall of Phothisat cave, Saraburi Province, Central Thailand, 7th-8th c. AD. Another significant object is a stone sculpture depicting the standing Buddha flanked by a pair of divinities over Vanaspati, the mythical creature from a mixed form of the Bull (the vehicle of Shiva), Garuda (the vehicle of Vishnu) and Hamsa (the vehicle of Brahma). This kind of sculpture was found in many sites of Dvaravati culture, e.g., in the Nakhon Pathom Province, Central Thailand, 9th-10th c. AD.

The images of Buddha standing on Vanaspati, the integrated form of three vehicles of the Three Supreme Hindu gods, of the communities reflect their knowledge of Hindu philosophy of the Trinity and their attempt to combine Hinduism with Buddhism. It is necessary to note that an image of this kind is not found in India.

Since the 15th century onwards the King of Thailand has been regarded as god Vishnu incarnated on earth. However, the Vishnu image and shrines were not built any more. On the other hand, Shiva was regarded as the protector of nature, of creatures on earth and of Buddhism. Thus, Shiva's shrine and its idol were built for worship. The knowledge of people about the four-faced Brahma was easily mixed with their knowledge about Avalogiteshavara (of Mahayana Buddhism) with his face turning to the four directions (to look after the creatures). Sculptures depicting four-faced figures were built with different kinds of material and forms in Buddhist temples, such as a stucco sculpture at the top of the entrance to the Wat Phra Si Ratana Mahathat Chaliang, Si Satchanalai District, Suthothai Province, 12th-13th c. AD, a gold disposal in the crypt of the Wat Ratchaburana, Phranakhon Si Ayutthaya Province, the early 15th c. AD. Thus these allow the two religious beliefs to intermingle without losing their identities.

5. Concept of adoption and adaptation of two main religions:

The concept is evidently implied in religious art of the two important religions which originated in India, i.e., Hinduism and Buddhism.

Hindu idols in Thailand in the 7th to 9th century were made in two ways: by holding the traditional concept of the Indian sculpture and by creating a new form. The phenomena reflects the different perceptions on art and beliefs of the indigenous people. For instance, the early image of Vishnu from Chaiya, Suratthani Province, Eastern coast of Southern Thailand, 5th c. AD, reflects the influence of South Indian tradition. The 8th century Vishnu in Yogasthanakamurti was found from the Phang-nga Province, Western Coast of Southern Thailand, is comparable to that found from South India, 7th c. AD.

The same tradition of making the four-faced Brahma in the two countries is exemplified by the sculpture of Brahma from Avantipura, Kashmir, India, AD 855-883, and Brahma from the Prasat Phanom Rung, Buriram Province, Northeast Thailand, 10th-11th c. AD.

The images of Brahma found in Thailand as well as images of Shiva and Vishnu reflect the tradition of worship of the three Supreme Divinities in Thailand in the 5th to the 12th c. AD.

However, the new idea of the indigenous artisan is exemplified by 11th century lintel from Nakhon Ratchasima Province, Northeast Thailand. This lintel depicts Shiva riding a bull flanked by Kartikeya riding a peacock and Ganesha riding an elephant, regardless of traditional practice, i.e. according to Indian mythology, where the vehicle of Ganesha is a mouse, not the elephant. The image of Vishnu in human form showing a male muscle according to anatomy which was made by local artisan reflects his new concept on artistic creation. This image was found at Khuan Phra Nua, Phangnga Province, west coast of Southern Thailand, 7th-8th c. AD.

The architectural form of the so-called Prasat or Prang in Thailand is comparable to that of Shikhara in South India, e.g. the Shiva temple at Kanchipuram, South India. This form of sanctuary built in Thailand since the 7th century had followed traditional Indian Shikharas. For instance, Prasat Phumpon, Surin Province, Northeastern Thailand, that is regarded as the earliest Hindu sanctuary found in Thailand, dated back to the 7th-8th c. AD. Though its upper structure was destroyed, the rest suggests to us the influence of the Indian Shikhara. This sanctuary is comparable to a Shikhara at Mamallapuram, South India, 7th c. AD.

The Indian Hindu sanctuary in the form of the Shikhara was completely present in the 10th-12th century in Thailand. This is shown by Prasat Narai Cheng Weng, Sakhon Nakhon Province, Northeast Thailand, 10th c. AD, and Prasat Phanom Rung, Buriram, Northeast Thailand, 11th-12th c. AD.

The form of Prasat, which originated from the Hindu Shikhara, was adopted by people of the Buddhist community to build a Buddhist temple in both Mahayanism and Theravada (Hinayanism). Before the 12th century there was no difference in the construction of the

Shikhara of the Hindu temple and of the Mahayana temple. The delicate form of the building developed by Thai artisans of Sukhothai in the 13th century replaced the stiff form of the Shikhara of the old time. For example, the Wat Si Sawai in the ancient town of Sukhothai was used as a Hindu temple in the 10th-11th c. AD, used as a Mahayana temple in the 12th c. AD, and used as a Theravada temple in the 13th-15th c. AD. The Prasat Hin Phimai, Nakhon Ratchasima Province was a Mahayana temple in the 11th-12th c. AD. The Wat Chao Chan, Si Satchanalai, Sukhothai Province, was a Mahayana temple in the13th c. AD and became a Theravada temple in the 13th-15th c. AD.

It is hard to find a complete building of a Buddhist temple of the early period in Thailand. However, one can compare from other art objects, such as a miniature stupa found in the Dvaravati site in Nakhon Pathom Province, Central Thailand, 7th-8th c. AD, or a Buddha sealing depicting the seated Buddha flanked by a pair of stupas from Yarang site, Pattani Province and from Phatthalung Province, Southern Thailand, 7th-8th c. AD. The shape of the above-said stupas is comparable to that found in the Vihara cave, India, 5th-6th c. AD. Thus the early Buddhist stupas in Thailand had an Indian model for their construction.

It is conjectured that the image of the Buddha standing in Tribhanga (triple flexion) from Nagapattinam, India, in the 7th-8th c. AD and from other sites inspired the artisans of Sukhothai to create the "Walking Buddha," the perfect image of the Buddha in typically Thai style in the 14th c. AD.

The art from Nalanda in the 10th-11th c. AD became a model of Buddhist art in Thailand in the same century. However, Thai craftsmen created "something new" in making Buddha images fit for their communal art appreciation. An image of the Buddha from Nalanda, Bihar, India, is comparable to that from Chiang Saen or Lanna art, which originated in the Northern territory of Thailand in the 13th-14th century. However, beyond the resemblance of the image, there is its own artistic aspect, i.e., the Buddha image of Lanna art has more broad shoulders and stronger muscles.

6. Impact of Indian philosophy through artwork:

The perception and cognition of Indian cosmology according to the Puranas of people in Thailand in the 10th to 12th century was expressed by engraving on pediment and lintel of the Hindu Shikhara. The two depictions: Yoganidra of Vishnu (the interval between the destruction and creation of the universe) and the Nataraja of Shiva or the dancing Shiva (the dynamic cycle of the universe) were noticeable. For example, the Yoganidra of Vishnu on the lintel of the Prasat Phanom Rung, Buriram Province, Northeast Thailand, 11th-12th c. AD, is comparable to that of Gupta art, at Deogarh, Uttar Pradesh, India, 6th c. AD. The movement of the universe is identified with the dancing of Shiva, the Nataraja. The Nataraja on the stone panel, late Chola, from South India, 12th c. AD, is comparable to that on the stone pediment of the Prasat Phanom Rung, Buriram Province, Northeast Thailand, 11th-12th c. AD. The bronze image of Nataraja from Chola art of South India, 12th c. AD is comparable to that from Nakhon Si Thammarat, South Thailand, 12th c. AD.

Hindu temples were built for the worship of the gods and to house their images; not only the Three Supreme Gods, but also the other gods and goddess. This can be seen in the integrated form of god and goddesses in the form of the Ardhanarishvara. An image of the Ardhanarishvara from Purapara, Bangladesh, 11th-12th c. AD, is comparable to that from Ubon Ratchathani, Thailand, 8th-9th c. AD. The philosophical concept of integration of a goddess into a god and of female power (Shakti) was expressed in artistic form. The female power in god was identified with the figure of Mahishasuramardini. For instance, Durga or Mahishasuramardini of Karnataka, South India, is comparable to that of the Prasat Hin Muang Khaek, Nakhon Ratchasima Province, Northeast Thailand, the 10th-11th c. AD.

The Pashupata yoga of Shaivism that was adopted by people in Thailand since the 7th c. AD had a lot of influence over artisans who made the idol, lintel or pediment for the Hindu temple. Therefore, the Thais of the 11th-12th century adopted the Samkhya and Yoga philosophies through Pashupata, the Shaivite sect. Furthermore, their understanding of the absolute truth in the philosophical teaching was illustrated on the lintel. Thus the depictions of "Formed Yogi and Formless Yogi" on the lintels were significantly discovered. With their wisdom of artistic expression, the Formed Yoga and Formless Yoga (Rupa Yoga and Arupa Yoga) was identified with the Formed Yogi and Formless Yogi carvings on the lintels and pediments of Hindu sanctuaries in the 11th-12th c. AD. For instance, Formed Yogis in Triangular Frames and three attitudes of Yogis contemplating in Yogasamadhi (meditation) on the lintel of the Prasat Ban Phluang, Surin Province, Northeast Thailand, 11th c. AD. Empty frames without the figure of the Yogi (Arupa Yogi who attains Arupa Yoga or Asamprajnayoga) can be seen on two lintels from the Prasat Muang Tam, Buriram Province, Northeast Thailand, 11th-12th c. AD.

The images of the seated Buddha in Padmasana were created in Sarnath, India, in the 5th c. AD and Mirpur Khas, Pakistan, 5th c. AD. The images, in the attitude, are comparable to that from the Prachinburi Province, Eastern Thailand, 8th-9th c. AD. The image is a representation of the event when Lord Buddha attained Enlightenment, for the lotus (Padma) represents spiritual purity. When the Lord became the Buddha, he was seated under the Bodhi Tree. People in Thailand followed the tradition of making artwork in the form of the Bodhi Tree. We have seen a terracotta Bodhi Tree from Mathura, Uttar Pradesh, India, c.100, which is with its characteristic fan-shaped leaves. The stucco Bodhi Tree from Sukhothai Province, 13th-14th century and the stone Bodhi Tree from Wat Khlong Salapun, Phra Nakhon Si Ayutthaya Province, 14th c. AD, are with their characteristic heart-shaped leaves. Thus art appreciation of people in India and of those in Thailand on the Bodhi Tree is not the same. We realize that the Bodhi Tree artworks of the two lands are distinctive in their style, but convey the same philosophical meaning. However, their perception on the philosophical meaning of the Bodhi Tree artwork constitutes two distinctive aspects; i.e., the Bodhi Tree with its characteristic fan-shaped leaves symbolizes the endless wisdom of the Enlightened One and the Bodhi Tree with its characteristic heart-shaped leaves symbolizes the mind as the core of Enlightenment.

It is conjectured that the art of making the image of Buddha followed the Indian practical concept since the propagation of

Buddhism from India to Thailand. One of the most popular postures of the image that people in Thailand made was the image of the Buddha in the Bhumisparsha-mudra (touching the Earth attitude) which has been recognized by the Thai as Maravijaya; the attitude of touching the earth is identified with the calling of the Earth, the goddess, to help Lord Buddha in fighting with Mara, the devil. The figure of the Goddess is created under the lotus seat of the Lord. She presses her hair to make water which drowns Mara's troops.

7. Interpretation on legends and myths in their own perception:

From the architectural elements of the Shikhara or the Prasat we have also seen the different perception of the Hindu in India and of the indigenous people in Thailand about the religious legends and myths. For instance, the Indian Shikhara has a bull figure as a decorative element on the roof, but the Shikhara (Prasat) in Thailand has a Naga figure instead, resulted from the indigenous belief, their primitive belief in the Naga.

The great Sanskrit epics from India, the Ramayana and the Mahabharata, were elaborately expressed on engraved lintels and pediments of many sanctuaries in Thailand between the 11th and the 12th century.

The variety of episodic depictions indicate the adoption of the Ramayana versions from various sources. For instance, the scene of the fight between the ogres and the monkeys on the stone lintel of the Prasat Hin Phimai, Nakhon Ratchasima Province, 11th-12th c. AD and the scene of Rama holding a bow to shoot arrows on the troops of the ogres on the stone lintel of the Prasat Hin Phimai, 11th-12th c. AD.

The Indian Ramayana was adopted and became a traditional art for sanctuary since the 11th-12th c. AD. It was rewritten by Thai scholars under the patronage of King Rama I in the late-18th century to become Thai literature, called the Ramakian. The literature inspired many artists to create mural paintings on the Buddhist halls of worship and/or in the ordination halls of many temples. At present, apart from the famous mural painting on the Ramakian at the Wat Phra Kaeo in the Royal Palace, a new technique of artistic creation is made by the Thai artisan. This is evident from the stucco bas-relief on the walls of the Wat Phananchoeng, Phra Nakhon Si Ayutthaya Province, 20th c. AD, depicting important scenes from the literature, e.g. the scene of Sita being abducted by Ravana, the scene of Hanuman asking the way to Lanka from Narada, the scene of Rama slaying Ravana.

The adoption and adaptation of the Mahabharata and the Puranas for artwork is seen in the following scenes carved on the lintel and pediment of many Prasats in the Northeast of Thailand: A lintel at Prasat Phanomrung, Buriram Province, Thailand, depicts Arjuna shooting a bird, instead of a fish, with a bow to wed Draupati, indicating the local adaptation of the Mahabharata for artwork. Images of Vishnu and His Incarnation were shown on the lintels and pediments of the Hindu and Buddhist Temples in the 10th-12th century, indicating the influence of the Puranas and the Mahabharata. For instance, a pediment depicting Krishna lifting up the Govardana mountain at Prasat Ban Phluang (Hindu temple), Surin Province, 11th c. AD; lintel of Prasat Muang Khaek (Hindu temple), Nakhon Ratchasima Province, 11th-12th c. AD, depicting Vamanavatar or Trivikrama; and the scene of churning the milky ocean for immortal ambrosia, lintel of Prasat Hin Phimai (Buddhist temple), Nakhon Ratchasima Province, Northeast Thailand, 11th-12th c. AD.

Under the influence of Buddhist legends and of the Hindu myths, these four zoomorphic creatures, elephant, simha (lion), naga (serpent) and garuda (divine birth) were counted in a new perception by people both in India and in Thailand. Sculptures of the zoomorphic creatures indicate that for the people in Thailand the non-domestic animal like the lion was supposed to be a creature of their acquaintance. The pendant with elephant figure as a amulet was found in the 1st century AD at the early port site in Thailand. People's feelings of love and fondness for the elephant, a domestic animal both in India and in Thailand, was enhanced with their feeling of adoration resulting from the belief of a divine elephant according to the legends and myths. Accordingly, elephant figures were made for the sake of religion and placed in the holy sites. The integration of Hindu gods into Buddhism is seen by the pediments depicting Indra riding Airavata, the divine elephant, placed over the entrance of the Buddhist temples. Different from Indian temples where figures of the bull were employed as a part of sanctuary, Naga figures have been employed instead in Thailand as a part of religious architecture, i.e. in the Shikhara, Shrine, Vihara, Uposatha. This resulted from combining the concept of the Naga in the legends and myths into the concept of serpent, the forefather-creature of the indigenous people. The divine birth, Garuda, attained the highest range of all zoomorphic figures since the worship of Vishnu, incarnated on earth as a king, has been practiced in the early 15th century. Garuda, the vehicle of Vishnu, becomes the emblem of the Royal family of Thailand. The Simha figure marks the Ashokan Pillar installed at the Buddhist holy places in India. In Thailand, figures of the Simha, as a divine guardian of Buddhism, have been placed in front of entrances to Buddhist temples since the 11th century onwards. The concept of the Simha came with the propagation of Buddhism to Thailand.

From the beginning of the earliest Ashokan stupa in India and the memorial pillar with the Simha on the top indicates that the clan of Lord Buddha will never perish. The Simha becomes the national emblem of India. Though the Simha is not a domestic animal in Thailand, it has been regarded as a religious symbol of Buddhism in the country.

Bibliography

Arya, Pandit Usharbudh, trans. *Yoga-Sutras of Patanjali with the Exposition of Vyasa*. Pennsylvania: The Himalayan International Institute of Yoga Science and Philosophy of the U.S.A., 1984.

Asthana, Shastri Prabha. *Mathura Kala* (Catalogue of Mathura Sculptures in National Museum). New Delhi: National Museum, Janpath, New Delhi: 1999.

Bhattacharya, Benoytosh. *The Indian Buddhist Iconography*. Calcutta: Firma K.L. Mukhopadhyay, 1968.

Boisselier, Jean. *The Heritage of Thai Sculpture*. Tokyo: Weatherhill, 1975.

Bowie, Theodore. & Griswold, A.B., and Diskul, MC Subhadradis. *The*

Sculpture of Thailand. Adelaide: Visual Arts Board, The Art Gallery of South Australia, 1976.

Charuk Nai Prathet Thai. *Charuk nai prathet thai lem nung: akson pallava lang pallava bhutthasatawat thi 12-14. lem sam: akson khom bhutthasatawat thi 15-16. lem si: akson khom bhutthasatawat thi 17-18*. (In Thai). Bangkok: Krom Silpakorn, 1986.

Chutiwongs, Nandana. "Trade Route and the Diffusion of Artistic Traditions in South and Southeast Asia" in *Ancient Trades and Cultural Contacts in Southeast Asia*, 3-37. Edited by Amara Srisuchat. Bangkok: The Office of the National Culture Commission, 1996.

Codrington, K. de B. "Indian Art and Archaeology" in *The Legacy of India*, 70-99. Oxford: Oxford University Press, 1951.

Damrong Rajanuphap, Somdet Krom Phraya. *Nithan Borankadi*. 15th ed. Bangkok: Bannakhan, 2000.

Daweewarn, Dawee. *Brahmanism in South-East Asia (from the earliest time to 1445 AD)*. New Delhi: Sterling Publishers, 1982.

Diskul, Subhadradis M. C. *Hindu Gods at Sukhothai*. Bangkok: White Lotus, 1990.

———. *Silpa Nai Prathet Thai* (Art in Thailand). (In Thai) 8th ed., Bangkok: Amarin, 1985.

Dawson, J. E. *Bronze Treasures of the National Museum*. New Delhi: National Museum, Janpath, 1999.

Dowson, John. *A Classical Dictionary of Hindu Mythology*. London: Routledge & Kegan Paul, 1972.

Dutt, M. N., trans. *Mahabharata*. Vol.1-7. Delhi: Parimal Publication, 1988.

Dutt, Romesh Chunder. *A History of Civilisation of Ancient India based on Sanakrit Literature*. Volume I –BC. 2000 to 320. Delhi: Vishal Publishers, 1972.

Feuerstein, Georg. *The Yoga Tradition*. Delhi: Motilal Banarsidass, 2002.

Fine Arts Department. *Guide to the National Museum Bangkok*. 4th edition, Bangkok: Office of Archaeology and National Museums, Fine Arts Department, 1999.

Frédéric, Louis. *Buddhism: Iconographic Guides*. Paris: Flammarion, 1995.

Gangadharan, N., trans. *The Agni Purana*. Part IV. Delhi: Motilal Banarsidass, 1987.

Ghose, Rajeshwari. *In the Footsteps of the Buddha: An iconic Journey from India to China*. Hong Kong: University Museum and Art Gallery, the University of Hong Kong, 1998.

Huntington, Susan L. *The Art of Ancient India*. New York: Weather Hill, 1985.

Indrawooth, Phasook. "Dvaravati: Concepts of State and Kingship." In *Sanskrit in Southeast Asia: The Harmonizing Factor of Cultures*. International Sanskrit Conference May 21-23, 2001, Bangkok, Thailand, 248-251. Bangkok: Sanskrit Studies Centre, 2003.

Knox, Robert. *Amaravati Buddhist Sculpture from the Great Stupa*. London: British Museum Press, 1992.

Kramrisch, Stella. *The Presence of Shiva*. Delhi: Motilal Banarsidass, 1981.

Krasuang Suksathikan, Krom Wichakan. *Phaet Sat Song Khro Phumpanna Thang Kanphaet Lae Moradok Thang Wannakam Khong Chat*. (In Thai). Bangkok: Krasuangsuksathikan, 1999.

Krom Silpakorn. *Phimai National Museum: The Center of Cultural Heritage in Northeastern Thailand*. Bangkok: Amarin Printing and Publishing, 1993.

———. *Nam Chom Phiphitthaphanthasathan Haeng Chat Prachinburi*.(In Thai). Bangkok: Krom Silpakorn, 1999.

Mani, Vettam. *Puranic Encyclopaedia*. Delhi: Motilal Banarsidass, 1993.

Masih, Y. *The Hindu Religious Thought* (3000 BC -200 AD). Delhi: Motilal Banarsidass, 1983.

McArthur, Meher. *Reading Buddhist Art*. London: Thames and Hudson, 2002.

Mongkutklaochaouhua, Phrabatsomdet. *Bo Koet Haeng Ramakian*. (In Thai), 7th ed. Bangkok: Silapabannakhan, 2001.

Na Nanagara, Prasert and Griswold, A. B. *Epigraphic and Historical Studies*. Bangkok: The Historical Society, 1992.

Niyada Laosunthon, ed. *Prachum Charuk Wat Phrachetuphon*. (In Thai). Bangkok: Khanasong Wat Phrachetuphon, 2001.

Niyogi, Puspa. *Buddhist Divinities*. New Delhi: Munshiram Manoharlal Publishers, 2001.

Pal, Pratapaditya. *Hindu Religion and Iconology According to the Tantrasara*. Los Angeles: Vichitra Press, 1981.

Phraphutthaloetlanapalai, Phrabatsomdet. 7th ed. *Bot Lakhon Ruang Ramakian*. (In Thai). Bangkok: Silapabannakhan, 2001.

Poussin, De La Vallée. "Buddhism" in *The Legacy of India*, 162-84. Oxford: Oxford University Press, 1951.

Prachum Phongsawadan Chabap Kanchanabhisek lem nung, lem sam, lem cet. Bangkok: Krom Silpakorn, Kong Wannakam Lae Prewattisat, 2002.

Prapandvidya, Chirapat. Brahmanism and Buddhism as Recorded in the Inscriptions of Sukhothai Period. 1826-2092 B.E. 1283-1594 A.D. In *Proceedings of The International Seminar on Brahmanism and Buddhism in Thailand*. August 19-21, 1994, Bangkok, 52- 62. Edited by Chirapat Prapandvidya Bangkok: Phragru Vamadevamuni Devasthan, Bangkok, 1996.

Radhakrishnan, S.. "Hinduism" in *The Legacy of India*, 256-286. Oxford: Oxford University Press, 1951.

Rao, T. A. Gopinatha. *Elements of Hindu Iconography*. Vol.1-Vol.2. Delhi: Motilal Banarsidass, 1997.

Ray, Himanshu P. *The Winds of Change : Buddhism and the Maritime Links of Early South Asia*. Delhi: Oxford University Press, 1994.

Sarkar, H. B. *Cultural Relations between India and Southeast Asian Countries*. Delhi: Indian Council for Cultural Relations and Motilal Banarsidass, 1985.

Shastri, Satyavrat. "Sanskrit Content in Thai Language." In *Sanskrit in Southeast Asia: The Harmonizing Factor of Cultures*. International Sanskrit Conference May 21-23, 2001, Bangkok, Thailand, 324-331. Bangkok: Sanskrit Studies Centre, 2003.

———. "Brahmanism in Sukhothai." In *Archaeology and History of Sukhothai*. Edited by Tharapong Srisuchat, Bangkok: The 6th Regional Office of Archaeology, Sukhothai, 2004.

Shearer, Alistair. *Buddha the Intelligent*. London: Thames and Hudson, 1997.

Sri Aurobindo. *The Synthesis of Yoga*. Sixth Reprint, Pondichery: Sri Ashram Trust, 1971.

Srisuchat, Amara. "Merchants, Merchandise, Markets: Archaeological Evidence in Thailand concerning Maritime Trade Interaction between Thailand and Other Countries." In *Ancient Trades and Cultural Contacts in Southeast Asia*, 237-274. Edited by Amara Srisuchat. Bangkok: The Office of the National Culture Commission, 1996.

———. *Major Events in History of Sukhothai*. Bangkok: Office of Environmental Policy and Planning, 2003.

———. "Yoga Philosophy in Secondary Thought: Tracing Back to Yoga in Thailand's Past." A Thesis Submitted in Partial Fulfillment of the Requirement for the Degree Doctor of Philosophy, Department of Oriental Languages, Graduate School, Silpakorn University. Bangkok: Silpakorn University, 2004.

Tagare, G. V., trans. *The Bhagavata Purana*. Part II. Delhi: Motilal Banarsidass, 1993.

Tripathy, S. S. *Buddhism and Other Religious Cults of South-east India*. Delhi: Sundeep Prakashan, 1988.

Symbolism and Development of the Triworld and Universe Paintings with Respect to Theravada Buddhism Concept as Shown on Thai Wall Mural Paintings

Sone Simatrang

❖

It is found after studies of the wall mural paintings all through the four regions of Thailand that those in the north, Esarn (northest), central and southern regions are of a different degree in design conceptualisation, design pattern and development. This is because of individual folk arts cultures and its different historical background which can be presented into three zones as follows: Lanna Cultural Zone (northern region), Esarn Cultural Zone (northeast region) and Ayuthya/Rattanakosin Cultural Zone which cover both the central and southern regions.

The conceptualisation of the Ayuthaya/Rattanakosin Cultural Zone will be highlighted in this study, which reflects those creative mural paintings during the 18th-20th century. The study will focus on the topic of Symbolism and Development of Triworld and Universe Paintings with Respect to Theravada Buddhism. The main aim of the study is as follows:

a) The design concept in creating human figures, animals,

architectural features, and landscape which lead to the meaningful symbols of the Triworld and Universe.

b) The concept in locating such murals on the back of the Buddha images in Buddhist temples.

Triworld and Universe Literature

Triworld and Universe are of Theravada Buddhism literature which is well-known among Southeast Asian countries where Theravada Buddhism is practiced since the 14th century: Thailand, Myanmar, Laos and Cambodia. In Thailand alone, ten different versions of such literature are kept in the National Library in Bangkok. After some of these texts were proofed, amended and translated from Pali into Thai, The National Library has published five of them as follows:

> Tribhumi-Khata, generally known as Tribhume-Pra Ruang, which is believed to be composed in 1346 AD by Praya Lithai one of the Sukhothai Kings who reigned during 1347-1376 AD.

Lokateepakasarn, composed by the Chief Patriach Metangkorn of Aranyawasi doctrine of the Sukhothai kingdom, who resided in Wat Ampawan (Wat Suan Mamuang) west of Sukhothai city. He was originally a Burmese monk who had studied the doctrine in Sri Lanka. While returning to Moulmein, this book was composed. The original copy cannot be traced; the copy kept in the National Library was etched on palm leafed in Khmer and Pali.

Lokabunyati, composed by Pra Sathadharma Kosa Thera, whose origin cannot be traced whether he was Burmese or Sri Lankan. It is assumed that the book may have been composed during the 9th century. The copy kept at the National Library was etched on palm leafed book in Burmese and Pali.

Jakravaldhipani, composed by Pra Sirimangkalajariya the Lanna monk who lived during 1477-1557 AD, while practicing monkhood at Wat Suan Kwan (presently called Wat Tamnak) outside Chiangmai city.

Tribhumi Lokavinijai, which was rearranged by Praya Dharmapreecha (Kaew) from the version of King Rama I of the Chakri Dynasty of Rattanakosin Kingdom (Bangkok) who reigned during 1782-1809 AD. The work was completed in 1811 AD.

Major Buddha Dharma Principles in Triworld and Universe Literature

All the five versions mentioned of the Triworld and Universe literature consisted of the three major principles of Buddha Dharma:

Triwatta, where the Buddha Dharma explains the three laws of Karma – Karma (performance, whether good or bad), Vibaka (result of such performance) and Reincarnation.

Trilaksana, where Buddha Dharma explains the three laws of Nature which consist of Anijam (uncertainty), Dhukkam (sorrow) and Anatta (not in existence, not being able to control).

Trisikha, where Buddha Dharma explains the three laws leading to a well conducted way of life. This consists of Sila (righteous way of life – physically right, verbally right and mentally right), Samadhi (mind at rest, concentration) and Punya (wisdom occurring by understanding the three laws of Nature).

To accentuate such principles mentioned above which influence a Buddhist, the Dharma is explained by analogical techniques to show the never-ending cycle of life in the Triworld (reincarnation).

Descriptive Information on the Concept of Triworld

Triworld means three levels of life which are Kamabhumi, Rupabhumi and Arupabhumi. Whatever level one is born to, everything depends on an individual's performance, good or bad. Beyond the three levels mentioned above, Nivarnabhumi is the state of living which is far from Kilesa in which one can get out of the cycle of reincarnation. Only those, who build their majesty resulting in enlightenment and reach the state of Sammasampotiyana to become the Buddha, Pajekabaddha and Arahanta, can reside in Nivarnabhumi. The description of the Triworld is as follows:

> Kamabhume or the lower state of life which enjoys Kama. Kama means desire, lust and craving, which is then divided into two, Kilesakama and Vastukama. Kilesakama passion and prejudices which cause desire consist of Raka (Sexual Desire), Lopa (Never Ending Greed) and Ijcha (Envy). Vastukama is where the five senses result in desire; Figures, Sounds, Scents, Taste and Physical Contact which can lead to self-satisfaction.

This Kamabhumi is divided into eleven levels; those living things who still crave for Kama shall carry on their cycle of life and death in these levels. Thus, it depends to their individual performance.

Rupabhumi: Medium State of Life to Enjoy Rupajana

Rupajana means practice in accordance to the disciplines of Sangkha (monks), Karavasa (human beings in general) and Tevada (devas, angels). Such practice is to take the four levels of Rupadharma into consideration, which are Patamajana, Dhutiyajana, Tatiyajana and Jatuttajana. Those who consistently practice these shall be incarnated as Brahman in Brahmaloka (world of Brahman). There are sixteen levels which are preferably called the "Rupabrahman, Sixteen Heaven Zones."

Arupaphumi: Higher State of Life Who Enjoys Arupajana

Arupajana means practice in accordance to the disciplines of Sangkha, Karavasa and Tevada. Such practice is to take the four levels of Arupdharma into consideration, starting from Akasananjayatanajana (taking the limitation of infinite space into consideration), Vinyarianjayatanajana (taking the limitation of infinite spirits into consideration), Akinjanyayatanajana (taking the limitation of infinite void into consideration) and Nevasanyanasanyatanajana (taking the limitation of infinite consciousness into consideration). Human beings, Tevada and Rupabrahman who have gone through such practice of the four Arupajana, shall be incarnated as Arupabrahman in Arupabhumi which is divided into four levels, preferably called "Arupabrahman, Four Upper Heaven Zones."

The Triworld consists of thiry-one minor zone levels as follows:
Kamabhumi: Eleven zone levels.

Zone 1:	Narakabhumi
Zone 2:	Tirajanabhumi
Zone 3:	Petubhumi
Zone 4:	Asurakayabhumi
Zone 5:	Manusyabhumi
Zone 6:	Jaturnaharajikabhumi
Zone 7:	Tawatingsabhumi
Zone 8:	Yarnabhumi
Zone 9:	Dusitabhumi
Zone 10:	Nimmanaratibhumi
Zone 11:	Paranimitavasawattibhumi

Rupabhumi: Sixteen zone levels.

Zone 12:	Brahmaparisajabhumi
Zone 13:	Brahmaparohitabhumi
Zone 14:	Mahabrahmabhumi
Zone 15:	Brahmaparittabhumi
Zone 16:	Brahmaaparnanabhumi
Zone 17:	Brahmaapasarabhumi
Zone 18:	Brahmaparittasupabhumi
Zone 19:	Brahmaaparnasupabhumi
Zone 20:	Brahmasupakinahabhumi
Zone 21:	Brahmavehapalabhumi
Zone 22:	Brahmaasanjlbhumi
Zone 23:	Brahmaavihabhumi
Zone 24:	Brahmaatappabhumi
Zone 25:	Brahmasahassabhumi
Zone 26:	Brahmasudhassibhumi
Zone 27:	Brahrnaakanitabhumi

Arupabhumi: Four zone levels.

Zone 28:	Akasananjayatanabhumi
Zone 29:	Vinyananjayatanabhumi
Zone 30:	Akinjanyayatanabhumi
Zone 31:	Nevasanyanasanyayatanabhumi

Descriptive Information on the Concept of Universe

There are two main concepts in every version mentioned previously of the Triworld and Universe literature: the belief in Triworld Existence and the belief in Universe Structure. While the two topics are clearly separate, the details are relevant. For example, the Triworld explains the major three states of life in the form of animals, human beings, angels and Brahman, their locations in the universe are also identified to visuals in the universe in a more perspective-oriented approach. The general descriptive information of the concept of universe is as follows:

The Beginning and Ending of the Universe

In accordance with the Buddha Dharma principles, all living things and other things on earth come under the laws of Nature i.e. Trilaksana. The beginning and end of the universe occurs in accordance with results and causes of the balancing of the four elements i.e. earth, water, air and fire. Such actions are infinite. The span between the beginning to the end of the universe is called Kappa.

The living things in each Kappa or a universe are identical; there are also Buddhas to set up disciplines for living beings in order to guide them to get out of Vattasangsara (infinite reincarnation). In each Kappa, there will be at least one to five Buddhas. In the present Kappa, four Buddhas have already happened on earth. The forthcoming Buddha, who will be the last for this Kappa, will be called the Pra Sriariyamatraya Buddha. Each series of disciplines set out by each Buddha will last for a certain period of time only; the disciplines of the present Buddha (Pra Srisakayamunibuddha) is set to last 5,000 years. After the decline of his disciplines, Pra Sriariyamettraya Buddha will emerge to set up new disciplines.

The Infinite Universe

Although there are infinite amounts of universe of identical shape, habitat, angles and Brahman, Buddha shall appear on our universe only to set out his disciplines. Our universe is called Mangkalaloka-jakarwalla, which is the centre, or Ananta-jakarwalla, which is divided into three orbital paths as follows:

Path 1, Jatiki-heta: There are 10,000 universes adjacent to each other orbiting around Mangkala-jakarwalla. Those angels and Brahmans in the 10,000 universe can sense the happening of each Buddha from His birth, pilgrimage, enlightenment, announcing the first sermon and His entering into Nirvana, and shall gather round to praise Buddha and as well as listen to His sermon.

Path 2, Anakheta: There are 100,000 universes orbiting around the Jatikheta. Although the power or the praise of Buddha can reach them, those angels and Brahman can not sense the happening of Buddha in the Mangkala-jakarwalla at all.

Path 3, Visayakheta: There are infinite numbers of universes orbiting on the outer rim of the Ananta-jakarwalla. However, the enlightenment of the Buddha can penetrate into such unknown region. Analogously, the enlightenment is by itself infinite.

Shape of Universe

Every universe contains the same shape throughout and consists of two main parts, i.e. earth and water, space or sky.

Earth and Water form a semispherical shape, where the flat part faces upwards. This semi-sphere stays afloat in the sea or space, by a turbulent storm support underneath. Every universe is floating adjacent to each other.

The floor of the universe is a circular plane, with the Sumeru Peak at the centre. The Peak is surrounded by Sattaboripandh (seven rings of mountain ranges); there is a sea called Sithundorn on every pair of mountain ranges. The Sumeru Peak in the highest peak of the universe and the other seven ringed peaks are lower respectively. Beyond the seventh range is the vast ocean surrounding these seven rings of mountains and seas. The boundary of the ocean starts from the edge of the seventh peak to the rim of the universe. In the vast ocean, there are four continents.

The names and shapes of these continents are: Burapavidheha Taweepa, the circular continent on the east; Amarakoyana Taweepa, the semicircular continent on the west; Uttaraguru Taweepa, the square continent on the north; and Chompu Teweepa, the triangular or elongated continent on the south. The last continent is the only one inhabited by human beings; the others are homes to non-human living things such as demigods who can levitate as the angels do.

In the sky, the Sun God rides his chariot drawn by Singhas (lions) and the Moon God rides his chariot drawn by white horses, orbiting in Taksinavatra manners (clockwise) around the Sumeru Peak. Ranges or Vimanas (angels' palaces) are afloat in the sky around the Peak.

On the top of the Peak resides Indra, the Supreme God which is called Tawatingsa Heaven; from the shoulder of the Peak to the edge of the universe is called Jatumaharajika Heaven. The Sumeru Peak is supported by three monolithic stones at its base, which also contain the city of the Asuras. Deep down, beyond the city of the Asuras, is the city of the Nagas.

Under Chompu Taweepa, there are eight layers of hell, which are called the Hell of Fire. The other hell is located among the adjacent space of the three universes, Naraka Lokantara (Hell of Extreme Cool), where its beings try hard to get away by climbing up the wall of the universe and are tortured by extreme cool and hunger.

Chompu Taweepa, the only continent where human beings live, consists of the Himalaya Forest where there are five mountains – Sutassanakoota (Golden Mountain), Jitrakoota (Jewels Mountain), Kalakoota (Jade Mountain), Kantamata (Sandalwood Mountain) and Krailasa (Silver Mountain). All these surround the Anodasa Lake which never dries up and is the origin of all watercourses on the continent. This lake has four outlets. Eastward the outlet symbolically represents lions, flows into the land where numerous lions roam about, and flows out to the ocean in the east. Westwards the outlet symbolically represents elephants, flows through the land where there are plenty of elephants, passing through to the ocean on the west. Northwards the outlet symbolically represents horses, flows through the land where there are plenty of horses, passing through the ocean on the north. Southwards the outlet symbolically represents cows, flows through the land where are plenty of cows which is the land where human beings live, passing through the ocean on the south.

Lake Anodasa has four landings: one at Kantamata Mountain for the Pajekabuddhas assembly for meditation practice. There, the elephant of Chattanta breed waits to serve those Pajekabuddhas. The second is for the angels bathing place; the third is for the fairies bathing enclosure and the fourth is a bathing place for rishis, gurus and noblemen.

The Basic Concept in Creating Work of Arts

There are two basics in creating work of arts: Perceptual Reality, the artist of this school respect natural laws of reality; and Conceptual Reality, the artists of this school do not follow the laws of nature but try to create designs symbolically to represent it.

Although the first concept lays emphasis on the reality of nature, its drawback is that the means of communication such as belief, dreams and imagination, which are surreal, cannot be expressed because of their abstract nature, while the latter concept can achieve abstract expression without having to rely on the reality of nature.

It is the freedom for any artist to choose their school of thoughts, and yet depend upon the context or the subject one would like to create. In creating the work of arts for the concept of Triworld and Universe, the second school is the only method to transfer its abstract views to its effective simplicity as well as the optimum expression on such artwork.

Methods in Creating Figures and Landscape in Thai Fine Arts

The Thai artist in those days had numerous methods to create figures and landscape called multi-dimensions on a single plane.

There are two meanings in the word Dimension which can be described thus: One being the physical dimensions of expression in the form of figures, such as the figure or face of a person showing sideways while his eye is seen as though it is looking directly in front. Further still, while the face is turned sideways, the body shows upfront, the hip faces sideways and the feet point to the opposite direction, etc.

The other dimension is the abstract dimension of time and event. The stories of Buddhist literatures which Thai artists express amalgamated whole events at a time onto a mural and the whole story was depicted.

A single plane means a common space or the same space that artists used for painting. For example, when the Thai artist wants to paint the story of the Buddha during his first encounter of the great renunciation, he would start at a corner of the desired space and paint the scene of Prince Siddhartha roaming through the park and sighting the four famous visions inspired by the devas for the Prince to feel compassion. On the same space, the artist would also paint the scene where the Prince returning from the park, visits his family and afterwards rides out of the city of Kabilavastu with Channa, his follower, for his great renunciation. However, Praya Maradhiraja tries to stop him. The whole story as mentioned would be painted on a space by the Thai artist who would set the spatial relationship as well as the amalgamation or the time dimension to be able to express the whole context completely. The example above is one of the creations of multi-dimensions on a single plane.

Three conditions cause the creation of figures and nature scenes of such multi-dimension on a single plane – one being the limited space, two, the overall length of the story that is far too long to be expressed on such limited space, and three, the need of freedom to cater to the artist's taste.

Multi-Dimension on a Single Plane Technique for Triworld and Universe Artwork

Mural paintings of Triworld and Universe in the Ayutthaya/Rattanakosin Cultural Zone were designed to paint on the space or the end wall of temples behind the main Buddha Image; the area allocated was approximately 8x8 metres. The area for the painting as previously explained is therefore far too small to put the whole story in.

Structurally and architecturally this side of wall is also divided into two parts, one part above the temple door right up to the ceiling lining and the other being the space between the backdoors. While on the top portion, the story normally started with the Manusyabhumi up to the Arupabhumi, the bottom would depict the Narakabhumi in general.

With respect to the technique of multi-dimensions on a single plane, Thai artists show their design of the Universe in a cross sectional pattern. The painting turns out symmetrical as the Sumeru is drawn at the centre and the seven rings of mountain ranges appear on both sides of it, instead of the Sumeru naturally being surrounded by seven layers of mountain ranges.

The Sumeru and Sattaboripandh mountains were painted on wave ornaments representing the Sithundorn Sea. Around the base of the Sumeru, giant fish representing the Ananta fish were drawn as mentioned in the story of Triworld.

Above the door, behind the Buddha Image in the Assembly or Ordination Hall, there is a band that is used to divide the mural into two zones. The bottom zone shows hell. The top zone is for the humans and devas. On the left and right at the end of the band, the edge turns upwards about 2-3 metres high and ends with the Vimanas at top of each band, representing the wall of Universe.

Beyond the Sattaboripan ranges, the paintings depict wave ornaments representing the vast ocean. Four symbolic continents are placed, two on each side. The arrangement of the four symbolic continents can be set out as below:

Pattern 1:	East Continent South Continent	North Continent Continent West
Pattern 2:	North Continent East Continent	West Continent South Continent
Pattern 3:	North Continent West Continent	East Continent South Continent
Pattern 4:	West Continent South Continent	North Continent East Continent

The South Continent is the Chompu Taweepa, the only continent which is inhabited by humans, the only place where the Buddha announces his doctrine.

The continent Chompu Taweepa is represented in the mural in two places at once. The first is normally presented in a triangle or oval form and placed in the ocean. The second is placed at the base of the

Sumeru depicting any city in Chompu Taweepa and tells the story of the Buddha's life.

The Narakabhumi (Hell Zones) consists of eight layers. Each layer has a main pit at the centre surrounded by sixteen pits in the four directions (north, east, west and south). The rim of each Hell layer consists of forty satellite pits, surrounding the Narakabhumi in a circle.

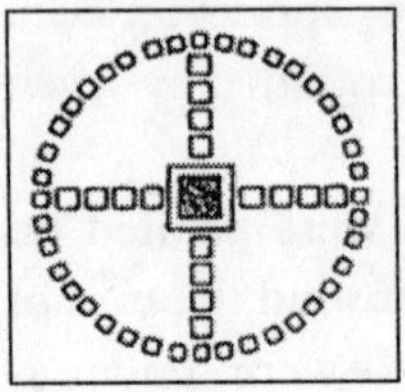

Therefore, in one Hell layer there are a total of fifty-seven pits. For presentation, the Thai artist draws tortured human faces and puts them in each pit. On the space left, the artist paints thc punishment to be meted to the visitors who come to the temple.

To this Narakabhumi scene, the figure of Pra Malai Thera was introduced. Pra Malai Kham Suad (the Chanting or Pra Malai) is used by Karavasa (normal people) after four monks have performed their chanting for the ceremony of the dead. The said literature was introduced by a Sri Lankan Monk during the 5th century AD. The oldest version found in Thailand is during the early Ayutthaya period and became most popular during the beginning of the Rattanakasin period (18th-19th century AD). Therefore, in this Narakabhumi scene, it is not uncommon to see a figure of a monk levitating in the air, one hand carrying a palm leaf fan and the other arm raised to his chest showing his intention to save mankind from sin, while a series of sinners look upon him with hope on their faces.

Pra Malai Thera is the being from Manusyabhumi while the sinners are from Narakabhumi. Such difference of Bhumi is the difference in a pattern of dimension. The technique of introducing different dimensions onto the same painting is the technique of creating multi-dimensions on a single plane, to show the difference in the dimensions of life. Thai artists have framed the Pra Malai Thera figure with the Fire "Kanok" pattern with the intent of accentuating the difference in the dimensions of life.

The design of location on the paintings of the Vimanas of Thao Jatumaharajika (the devas who guard the four directions) has been done in the same manner as the Sumeru idea by flattening the actual perspective to a two dimensional view so that the viewers can see all the four Vimanas on a single plane. Thus, the technique is another exercise of multi-dimension on a single plane.

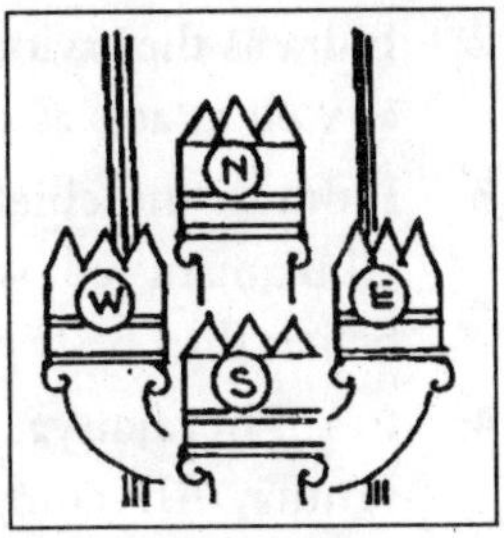

In the design, the Sun and Moon Gods are symbolically represented as two types:

Type 1: A circle of red with the Sun God on his chariot inset by lions. The Sun God is also red. And, a circle of white with the Moon God on his chariot inset by white horses. Some paintings also show a white rabbit sitting on the back of the chariot. It is believed that in one of the Buddha's reincarnated lives, as mentioned in the Attakhalapalijataka, Chapter 316, he was born as the white rabbit.

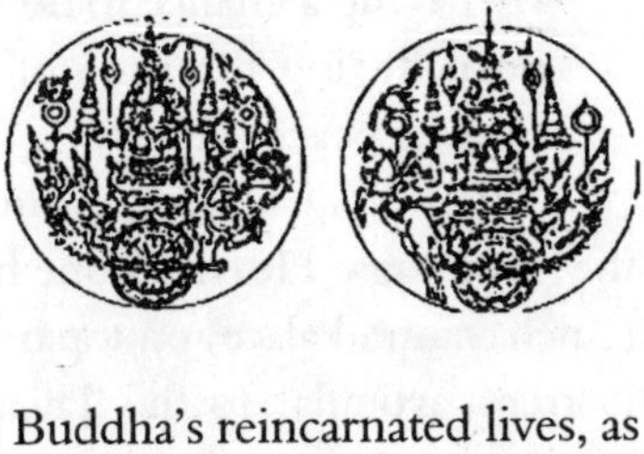

Type 2: A circle of red inset with a peacock and a circle of white inset with a rabbit representing the Sun God and the Moon God respectively. The same reason, as mentioned in the Attakhatapalijataka, Chapter 491, applies here for the use of the peacock and the rabbit.

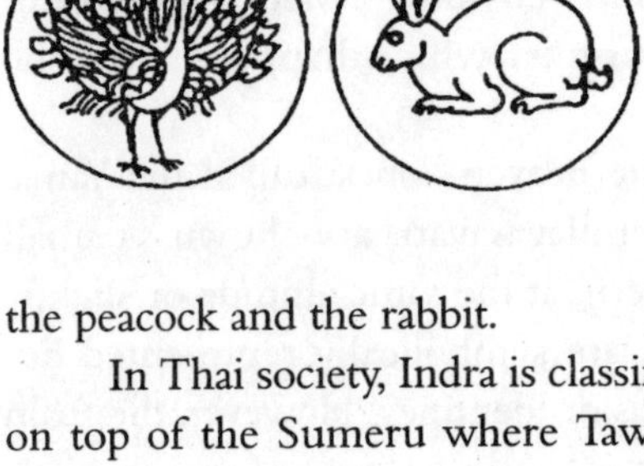

In Thai society, Indra is classified as the supreme God who lives on top of the Sumeru where Tawatingsa Heaven is situated. Most

Thais are accustomed to this Heaven zone because of the following four reasons:

1: To be born as Indra is the result of Karma. One who donates much from his wealth while he is human, will be born as Indra in this zone when his time on earth has ceased.

2: Indra as the saviour of the Buddhists who face Dukkha (sorrow) as well as acts as a guardian over religious rituals.

3: Indra as the chief of the devas during the construction of the Chulamani Jedi where the hair and the tooth relic of Buddha is believed to be kept in this Tawalingsa Heaven.

4: Pra Therajanya, the Sri Lankan highbrow, during the 5th century AD composed the story of Pra Malai to reinforce the law of Karma believers that any Buddhist who performs good deeds shall be born in the Tawatingsa Heaven. With such merit, he will then have a chance to pay respect to the Chulamani Jedi. By having a chance to do so, when next reincarnated, he will be born during the time of Pra Sriariyamettraibuddha, which is time of peace.

Hence, Thai artists would particularly stress the importance of the Tawatingsa Heaven Zone by drawing the oversize Palace of Indra (Paichayantra Palace) on top of the Sumeru Peak with the Parijati tree (a tree particular to the Tawatingsa Heaven) on one side and the Chulamani Jedi on the other side. Nearby, around Chulamani Jedi, it is popular to depict Pra Malai levitating, about to pay respect to the Jedi or preaching to the devas.

On the sides of Chulamani Jedi, a pair of crocodile flags and centipede flags are popurlarly shown. These flags symbolically represent one of the Thai religious customs called Todd Kratin (offerrings made to Buddhist monks) which happens after the Buddhist Lent day of every year.

The Vimanas of devas in the heaven zones, called the Yama, Dusita, Nimmanarati and Paranimilavasavati, are shown as small Vimanas floating around the Sumeru, at the same altitude or slightly higher. In the Vimana, the devas are symbolically represented but cannot be identified by their shapes or identities. However, the main aim is to represent the actual quantity of Vimanas according to the belief and the text.

The sixteen Vimanas for the Brahmans in Rupabrahman Heaven Zone are shown as the highest order or Vimanas. In the Vimana are seated four-faced Brahmans, whose name and identity are not known. However, the main aim is to represent the actual quantity of the Vimanas according to the belief and the text.

The four Vimanas for Brahman in the Arupabrahman Heaven Zone are shown as huge Vimanas floating among or above those in the Rupabrahman Heaven Zone. In the Vimana is seated a circular stone, which symbolically represents the Arupabrahman.

Development in Landscape Design for Triworld and Universe

The development in landscape design for Triworld and Universe painting can be divided into three styles:

Style 1: During the decline of the Ayutthaya Period until the rise of the Rattanakosin Period (c. 17th-18th century AD). The highlight of the painting was the emphasis on the Paichayantra Palace, Parijati Tree and Chulamani Jedi in the Tawatingsa Heaven Zone, as well as to introduce a part of Buddha's life in abstract form by depicting him when he goes to preach to his mother and the devas during the Lent period. One of the examples of such expression is shown at Wat Srakate in Bangkok (c. 19th century AD).

Style 2: During mid-19th to early 20th century AD. Elements similar to the previous style can be detected, as well as extra elements introduced such as the crystal (diamond) ladder, the silver ladder and the gold ladder spanning over from the Tawatingsa Heaven Zone onto the Chompu Taweepa, with the devas and Brahmans levitating about the steps. This style can be seen at the temple of Wat Suwannaram, Bangkok Noi, Bangkok (c. end of 19th century AD).

Style 3: The basic element, although similar to the previous styles, omits certain main continents. The main differences are: only the Chulamani Jedi is shown on top of the Sumeru Peak; there is neither the Paichayantra Palace nor the Parijati Tree. Such omissions highlight the development which happen where local belief somehow differed.

This example or the style is seen at Wat Nong Soong Yang, Saraburi. This particular mural was painted during early 19th century AD.

Reasons of Placing Triworld and Universe Mural Paintings on the Backwall of the Temple behind the Buddha Image

Although the ancient intentions of these Thai artists are not known, after a study and observation of the mural paintings as well as architectural reasons, two assumptions may be reached:

First, the scene of the Triworld and Universe is an important element architecturally, especially being the main Factor to "fill in" the blank space of the temple. The back space, after painting, can then represent the Tawatingsa Heaven Zone, as well as the who'.; atmosphere in the temple. And if this hypothesis is correct, it means that the people who come to the temple are in the dimension of the make-believe Tawatingsa Heaven Zone.

Second, the scene of Triworld and Universe is a means of architectural factor to create spatial relationship in the temple with the Main Buddha Image and also becomes artistically impressive,

---

NOTE: The drawing is not copied from any particular Wat but made by Sone Simatrang by amalgamating the general layout from several Wats such as: Wat Dusitaram Dhonburi, Wat Suwarnnaram Dhonburi, Wat Rajasitharam Dhonburi and Wat Yai Indharam Cholburi.

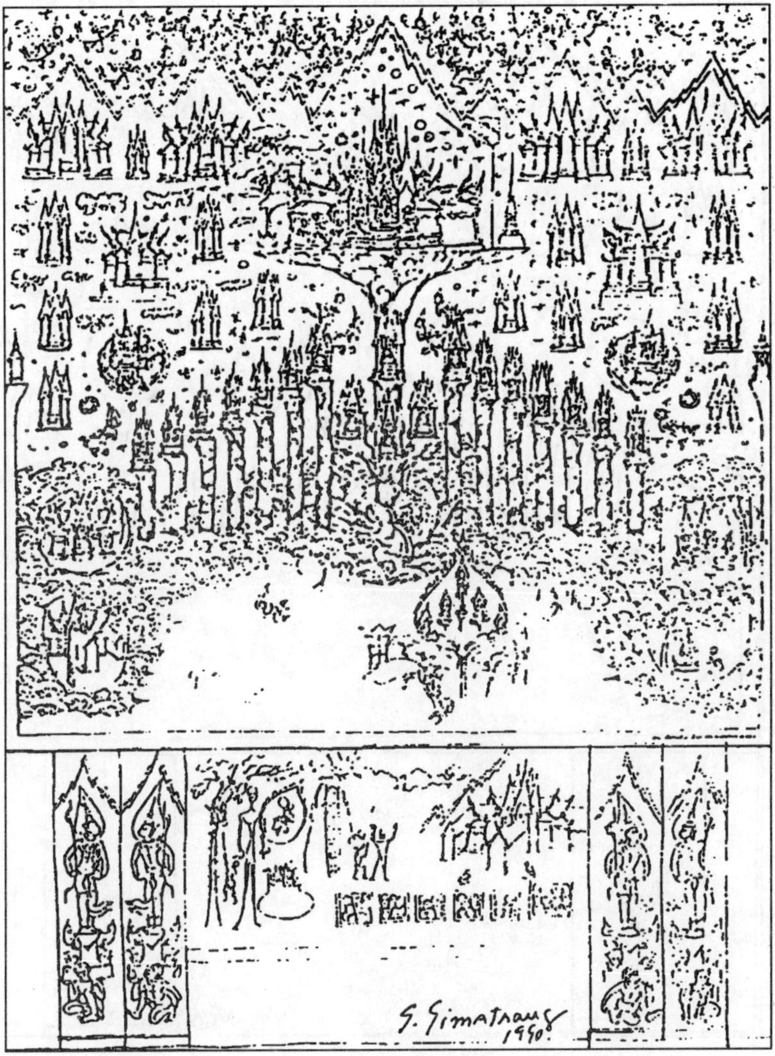

Illustration No. 1:

Picture of Triworld and Universe as collected from Wats built during the period of King Rama I-II.

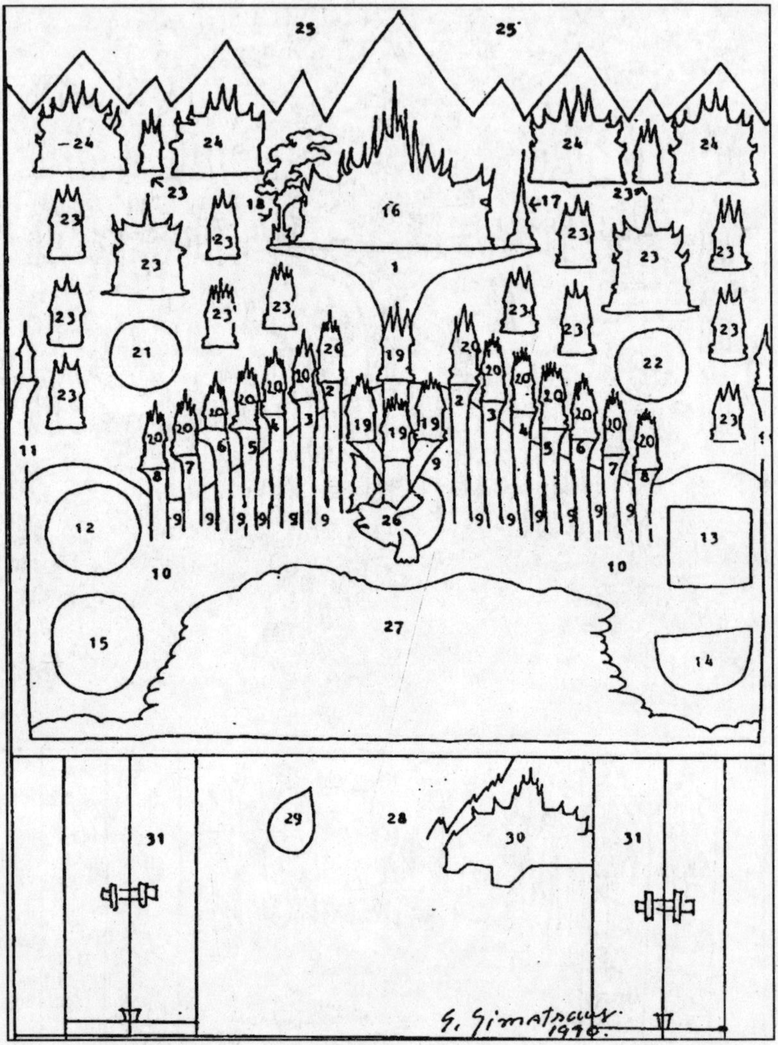

Illustration No. 2:

Picture of Triworld and Universe as collected from Wats built during the period of King Rama I-II.

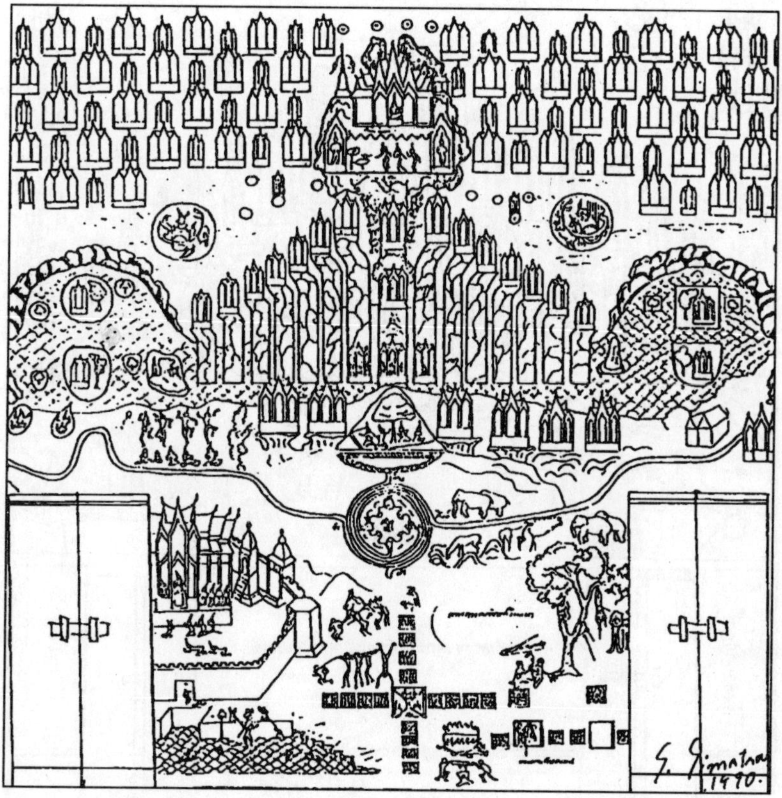

Illustration No. 3:

Picture of Triworld and Universe on mural at the Ordination Hall of Wat Sra-Ket, Bangkok. Dated early 24th century BE.

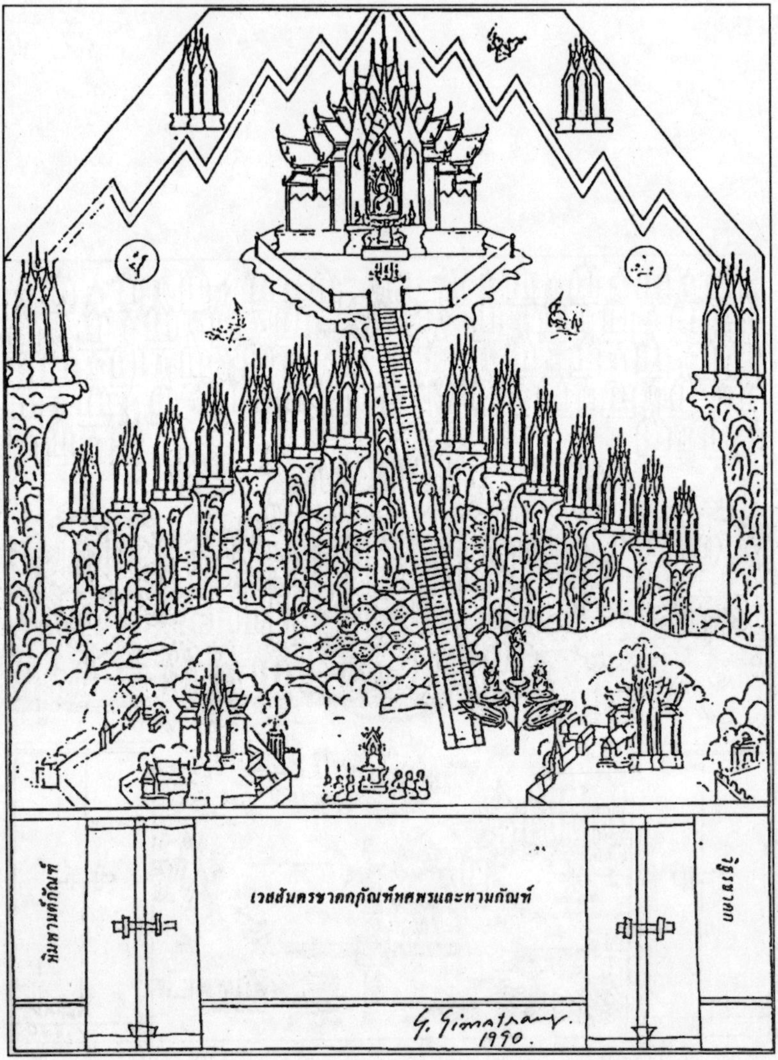

Illustration No. 4:

Picture of Triworld and Universe on mural at the Ordination Hall of Wat Suwannaram. Bangkok, Dated late 24th century BE.

Illustration No. 5:

Picture of Triworld and Universe on mural at the Ordination Hall of Wat Nong-Yang-Sung, Sraburi Provincd, dated early 25th century BE.

Illustration No. 1:

The drawing of Triworld and Universe are collected from the mural of many temples built during the period of King Rama I-II.

Illustration No. 2:

Layout of Triworld and Universe are collected from the mural of many temples built during the period of King Rama I-II.

Explanation of Illustrations No.1 & 2:

1: Sumeru Peak (Central Universe Core) 84,000 Yochana above the sea and 84,00 Yochana below the sea.

2: Yukhantara Peak (Sattaboripan 1st ring) 42,000 Yochana above the sea and 42,000 Yochana below the sea.

3: Isinthorn Peak (Sattaboripan 2nd ring) 21,000 Yochana above the sea and 21,000 Yochana below the sea.

4: Karavik Peak (Sattaboripan 3rd ring) 10,500 Yochana above the sea and 10,500 Yochana below the sea.

5: Sudhassana Peak (Satlaboripan 4th ring) 5,250 Yochana above the sea and 5,250 Yochana below the sea.

6: Nemindhara Peak (Sattaboripan Sth ring) 2,625 Yochana above the sea and 2,625 Yochana below the sea.

7: Vrnantaka Peak (Sallaboripan 6th ring) 1,312.5 Yochana above the sea and 1,312.5 Yochana below the sea.

8: Assakanna Peak (Sattaboripan 7th ring) 656,25 Yochana above the sea and 656-25 below the sea.

9: Sitthundorn River (Fresh water) widest part is 84,000 Yochana and narrows down to 1,312.5 Yochana.

10: The Ocean (Salt water) from Assakanna Mountain to the Universe Wall is 309,694 Yochana.

11: The Universe Wall (the edge of Universe) 82,000 Yochana above the ocean and 82,000 Yochana below the ocean.

12: Burapavitheha Taweepa (Eastern Continent) round shape with its diameter of 7,000 Yochana.

13: Uttraguru Taweepa (Northern Continent) square shape with 7,000 Yochana long.

14: Amorakoyana Taweepa (Western Continent) semi-circular shape with diameter of 7,000 Yochana.

15: Chompu Taweepa (Southern Continent) elongated or triangular shape with 10,000 Yochana wide.

16: Paichayantra Palace. The Vimana of Indra, the supreme God of the Tawatingsa Heaven.

17: Chulamani Jedi where Buddha's hair and teeth are placed, on the Tawatingsa Heaven.

18: Parijati Tree. The tree on Tawatingsa Heaven.

19: The Vimana of Ti-Tao Chatulokabala, the supreme God of Chatumaharajika Heaven.

20: Vimanas Of Thao Chatulokabalas Devas.

21: Suriyadheppabutra. The Sun God roaming clockwise in the chariot drawn by lions around the Sumeru.

22: Chantaradheppabutra. The Moon God in the chariot drawn by white horses.

23: Vimanas of Sixteen Zones of Rupabrahman.

24: Vimanas of Four Zones of Arupabrahman.

25: Sages and Gurus levitate to greet Buddha.

26: Ananta Fish. One of seven kinds of giant fish in the ocean.

27: Habitants and City in Chompu Taweepa.

28: Hell Scene (Narakabhumi). There are eight pits of hell, each pit consists of sixteen smaller pits, also including other forty pits in each major pit. The major pits namely: Sanjeepanaraka, Kalasuttanaraka, Sanghatanaraka, Roruvanaraka, Maharoruvanaraka, Tapanaraka, Mahatapanaraka and Mahaavelji.

29: Pra Malai Visits Hell. Pra Malai is the last Arahanta in Sri Lankan and Thai belief. He was the one who introduced the belief in the next Buddha, Pra Siariyamettrai.

30: Praya Yommaraja Palace while judging sinners.

31: The Temple Backdoor.

Illustration No. 3:

Picture of Triworld and Universe on mural at the Ordination Hall or Wat Sra-Kct, Bangkok. dated early 24th century BE.

Illustration No. 4:

Picture of Triworld and Universe on mural at the Ordination Hall of Wat Suwannaram, Bangkok, dated late 24th century BE.

Illustration No. 5:

Picture of Triworld and Universe on mural at the Ordination Hall or Wat Nong-Yang-Sung, Sraburi Province, dated early 25th century BE.

Bibliography

Jakravaldhipani. Pra Strimangkalajariya composed this in Pali during 1520 AD, and it was translated into Thai by Thongyoi Saensinchai (Bangkok: National Library, Fine Arts Department, 1980).

Tripume Pra Ruang. Composed by Praya Lithai (1345 AD). Copied and etched on palm leaf by Pra Maha Chuay or Wat Paknam (1778 AD). First Publication in 1912 for the cremation ceremony of Prachao Boromawongther Praong Prasarn Srisai Praongchao Prapai Srisaad (Bangkok: Vajirayana Library).

Tripume-Khata. Composed by Triphume Pra Ruang but re-checked by the National Library; third publication for seminar in Triphum Pra Ruang during the 700 years Thai Alphabet Celebration 19- 21 December 1983, National Library (Bangkok: National Library, 1983).

Tripume-Khata. Simplified version by the ASEAN Literature Committee (Bangkok: The ASEAN Literature and Information Committee).

Tripume-Lanna. The Lanna version, transferred from a palm leaf version onto paper by Assistant Professor Udom Roongruangsri; first publication 250 copies in Roneo form (Chiengmai; Lanna Arts and Culture Unit, Faculty of Humanities, Chiengmai University, 1981).

Tripumelokayinuaya Khata. Edited by Praya Dharmapreccha (Kaew) in 1802 AD as directed by King Rama I, checked and verified by the Literature and History Division, Fine Arts Department, 3 volumes per set (Bangkok: Fine Arts Department, 1977).

Lokatllpakasarn. Composed by the Chief Patriarch Matangkorn towards the end of the 14th century AD at Moulmein, Myanmar; checked and verified by the National Library (Bangkok: Fine Arts Department).

Lokabanyati. Composer not known, assumed composed towards the end of the14th century AD in Myanmar; checked and verified by the National Library (Bangkok: Fine Arts Department, 1985).

Satienkosate. Pen name *Tripume Retold* third publication (Bangkok: Klangwidhaya Printing, 1975).

Simatrang, Sone. *Rattanakosin Mural Paintings*. Published for the exhibition on *Photography on Thai Mural Paintings* at Khon Kaen University, 14-29 December 1979 (Bangkok: Arts and Culture Promotion Committee, Khon Kean University, 1979).

———. *Lanna Mural Paintings* (Research on the same name as supported by the Toyota Foundation (Bangkok: Silpakorn University, 1983).

Phirasri, Silpa. *Development of Wall Mural Paintings In Thailand* as translated by M. C. Subathara dis Diskul (Bangkok: Fine Arts Department 1959).

Fine Arts Department. *Brief On The Seminar Of Triphum Khata Pra Ruang* as arranged by the ASEAN COCI on 28 February-1 March 1983 at Vajiravudbanusorn Hall, National Library (Bangkok: Fine Arts Department, 1983).

———. *Conclusion on Tripume Pra Ruang Simanar* published for 700 years of Thai Alphabets Celebration (Bangkok: Fine Arts Department, 1984).

Indo-Thai Relations after World War II

NOPHADOL CHARTPRASERT

❖

Indian and Thai civilizations have been linked for more than 2000 years in religious, linguistic and socio-economic dimensions. Consequently, India's culture permeated almost every aspect of Thai culture. Therefore, although the political and economic relationships between Thailand and India were occasionally interrupted, the relationship between Thai and Indian people has been continuously cordial. This paper will describe and analyze Indo-Thai relations after World War II, especially in its political and economic dimensions.

When India got independence on 15 August 1947, the Indian government set out to improve its relations with the neighboring countries (Jha, 1979: 134). Thailand was amongst the very first countries that established diplomatic relations with India in 1947. Thanat Khoman became the first Thai Charge d'Affaires to Delhi (Gupta, 1997: 20). India set up a full-fledged Embassy in Thailand in 1951. This was reciprocated (Jha, 1979: 134). Thailand had to pay £5,224,220 to Great Britain by way of compensation under the Peace Treaty of January 1946. India's share of this sum was £104,484. However, as soon as it gained its freedom from British rule, India waived the compensation due to it (Jha, 1979: 134). This gesture indicated that India preferred to establish a cordial relationship with Thailand.

However, before the late 1980s, Indo-Thai political relations had not developed much. The different points of view between

Thailand and India towards the Cold War, globally and regionally, can be considered as a main reason.

India believed that the moral imperatives and principles that had guided the Allies to victory in the World War II would lead to a better world for all humanity. India felt very strongly that a new world order was necessary and all countries must have the right and ability to make their independent judgments on various world issues (Gupta, 1997: 21). After India had become independent, it decided to implement an independent and active non-aligned foreign policy. India placed itself outside the power blocs and refused to join any military pact sponsored by any of the superpowers (Kaul, 2001: 41).

Thailand's policy was clearly different from India's policy. Field Marshal Pibulsongkram was one of the Asian leaders to support the policy of military alignments advocated by the United States to counter Communist activities. He actively supported the Southeast Asia Treaty Organization (SEATO) and offered Bangkok as its headquarters (Jha, 1979: 134-35). The then widely-held domino theory suggested that if Thailand could be maintained as a strong and prosperous anticommunist bulwark, the growing communist threat in Southeast Asia might be checked and contained (National Identity Board, 2000: 206).

On the other hand, the Indian Prime Minister, Jawaharlal Nehru, did not support the existence of SEATO. In a speech during a debate on foreign affairs in the Lower House of the Indian Parliament in 1954, he said that if India had participated in the Manila Conference, it would have meant India's giving up its basic policy of non-alignment. Moreover, India's participation could have affected its position as the Chairman of the International Control Commission in Indochina. He also challenged the usefulness of SEATO, and said that it had only added to the tension in Southeast Asia (Jha, 1979: 135).

Pakistan, which had a territorial conflict with India, supported the SEATO. By virtue of its membership of the SEATO, it automatically became the recipient of military and political support from the eight member nations of the Manila Pact, including Thailand (Jha, 1979: 135). India believed that Pakistan did not really fear the threat from China, but joined the SEATO in order to confront India (Nibhatsukit, 1992: 62).

In addition, the Thai and Indian views towards the Korean and the Vietnam Wars were different. For the Korean War, the Indian government did not support the United States' mission in the war and called for peaceful resolution, but the Thai government strongly supported the Americans and sent Thai forces to assist the South Koreans. In the case of the Vietnam War, the Thai government believed that it was a war between North and South Vietnam which clearly presented the aggression of North Vietnam which had to be resisted by the forces, but the Indian government believed that a peaceful solution would materialize (Nibhatsukit, 1992: 54-60).

Even though political relations between Thailand and India had not improved much during the Cold War, economic cooperation between the two countries had continued. For instance, in 1955 the Thai Ambassador to India presented 300 tons of rice for the relief of the flood-affected areas in Northeast India. Later, in 1956, India and Thailand signed an Air Traffic Agreement in Bangkok (Jha, 1979: 135).

Tension developed in Indo-Thai relations again when Thailand protested against the United States' decision to send 100,000 tons of rice to India under a PL480 agreement in May 1960. The Thai Foreign Minister, Thanat Khoman, disclosed that Thailand had been negotiating with India the sale of 100,000 to 200,000 tons of rice. He charged that the Indo-US agreement on the supply of foodstuffs in May 1960 was responsible for the decline in the price of Thai rice. However, the Government of India and the United States Embassy in India refuted the Thai charge. They said that Thailand was not a regular supplier of rice to India; that in the past eight years, India had not imported any rice from Thailand; and that the fall in the price of Thai rice was on account of increased production of rice in Burma, Japan, and South Vietnam (Jha, 1979: 135-36).

Indo-Thai relations faced another problem when India liberated Goa, Daman, and Diu from the colonial rule of Portugal in December 1961. In this case, the Thai Foreign Minister expressed his disagreement towards India's action (Jha, 1979: 136). Notwithstanding all this, India expressed an interest in buying Thai rice when in March 1962 Burma put restrictions on the export of rice and other commodities

(Jha, 1979: 136). However, the Sino-Indian border conflict in 1962 altered the Thai policy towards India. Thailand extended its full support to India in the fight against China. India received a message of support and sympathy from the Prime Minister of Thailand, Field Marshal Sarit Thanarat. He remarked in October 1962 that Thailand might assist India at the United Nations in the war against China (Majumdar, 1982: 57). In addition, in an interview to a special correspondent of the Press Trust of India, Thanat Khoman said that the future of both countries lay in collective security. India and Thailand should join hands, not to work against anyone in particular, but to defeat aggression wherever possible. If India, Thailand, and some other countries of the region joined hands to promote unity, solidarity, and cooperation in Asia, that would be the best possible service by them to the people of Asia (Jha, 1979: 137).

Indo-Thai economic relations were sustained and improved during the 1960s. In 1964, India had entered into agreements with Thailand and Cambodia for the purchase of 25,000 tons of rice from each of them. This formal rice agreement was the first that India signed with Thailand after achieving its independence. Later, on 21 June 1965, India and Thailand were linked by a direct radio-telephone service (Jha, 1979: 137). India signed its second rice agreement with Thailand in 1966 and bought 150,000 tons of rice on a Government-to-Government basis (Jha, 1979: 137-38).

In the same year, Zakir Husain, then India's Vice President, paid a visit to Thailand from 8 to 10 October 1966. At a banquet given by the Thai Prime Minister, Field Marshal Thanom Kittikachorn, India's Vice President said that he came to Thailand as India's messenger of goodwill. He looked forward to increasing cooperation between the two countries, which, according to him, had walked together through the avenues of history, sharing common dreams and thoughts (Jha, 1979: 138). A few months later, in January 1967, the Indian Foreign Minister, Ali Currim Changla, also visited Thailand (Nibhatsukit, 1992: 85).

A. L. Dias, the Secretary to the Government of India in the Ministry of Food, went to Bangkok in June 1968 to negotiate yet another purchase of rice. On his return to New Delhi on 10 June

1968, he disclosed that Thailand had agreed to supply 80,000 tons of rice to India on a Government-to-Government account (Jha, 1979: 138).

A Thai trade delegation visited India on 21 February 1969 and held negotiations with the Indian Minister for Foreign Trade, B. R. Bhagat. A joint communiqué issued on 23 February 1969 said that India was in a position to export to Thailand a wide range of manufactured products, such as machinery and machine tools, rails and rail-track accessories, transmission lines, telecommunication equipment, and structural steel. In return, Thailand would supply rice and other agricultural commodities. The communiqué added that a close cooperation between the two countries was needed. The attempt was not only to strengthen the existing pattern of cooperation, but also to evolve new ones (Jha, 1979: 138-39).

Immediately thereafter, India signed an agreement with Thailand on 2 May 1969 to buy 75,000 tons of rice on a Government-to-Government basis to be delivered in monthly shipments of 20,000 tons. Just four months after signing this agreement, on 2 September 1969, there came yet another rice agreement. Under this agreement Thailand agreed to supply 25,000 tons of parboiled rice. The total export of rice to India in 1969 was 100,000 tons, about $ 240 million in value (Jha, 1979 : 139).

India's policy towards Southeast Asia was again put to test when Prince Narodom Sihanouk of Cambodia was ousted by a military coup in March 1970. The Thai government strongly supported the new regime in Cambodia. After Sihanouk's overthrow, most countries which were on friendly terms with Cambodia, closed down their embassies in Phnom Penh. But India and USSR kept their embassies in Phnom Penh and maintained diplomatic relations with the Lon Nol government (Majumdar, 1982 : 109-10). Since Thailand strongly supported the Lon Nol regime, therefore it is understandable that the Thai leader appreciated India's policy towards Cambodia.

In the 1970s, the relationship between Thailand and India became more cordial. India signed a truly comprehensive agreement in September 1970. This was a three-year pact under which Thailand agreed to sell 400,000 tons of rice a year to India. Thailand on its part agreed to buy plant equipment and machinery of equivalent value from India for state enterprises and government organizations under competitive international tenders (Jha, 1979: 139). In 1972, V. V. Giri became the first President of India who visited Thailand (Nibhatsukit, 1992: 85). The maritime boundary was amicably delimited in 1973 and a Cultural Agreement was signed in 1977 (Gupta, 1997: 22). In 1978, the Deputy Prime Minister and Minister of Foreign Affairs from Thailand visited India. Later in 1979, General Kriengsak Chamanand, on the way back from Moscow, made a brief visit in India and had a brief discussion with Indian Prime Minister, Moraji Desai (Nibhatsukit, 1992: 85).

In the early 1980s, India relations with Thailand faced a new serious problem when the Indian government recognized the Heng Samrin regime in Cambodia. With Thailand as a frontline state against the Vietnamese occupation of Cambodia, Indo-Thai relations were far from amicable (Chongkittavorn, 1997: A4). The trade between Thailand and India had been sustained during the 1980s with regard to the Indo-Thai relations on the economic front, but the volumes had not increased significantly.

When the international system was shifting away from polarized system of the Cold War in the mid-1980s, the artificial obstacles that had been created in Indo-Thai relations fell away. Since the mid-1980s, the exchanges of high level visits have been sustained.

His Royal Highness Crown Prince Maha Vajiralongkorn visited India twice in April 1992 and December 1998. Her Royal Highness Princess Maha Chakri Sirindhorn visited India five times in March 1987, December 1996, March 2001, April 2001 and February to March 2005. Her Royal Highness Princess Chulabhorn visited India thrice – from November to December 1996, in January 2004 and in November 2004 (Ministry of Foreign Affairs, 2005).

Prime Minister Rajiv Gandhi paid the first-ever official visit of an Indian Prime Minister to Thailand in 1986. General Chatichai Choonhavan also paid the first ever official visit of a Thai Prime Minister to India in 1989 (Gupta, 1997: 22-23). After these official visits were successfully made by Indian and Thai Prime Ministers, the visits by the head of governments from both countries have continuously followed. In April 1993, Prime Minister Narasimha Rao visited Thailand (Gupta, 1997: 23). Prime Minister Taksin Shinawatra visited India thrice – in 2001, 2002 and 2005. During the visit to India by the Thai Prime Minister in 2001, the two sides agreed to intensify bilateral cooperation in advanced technology, study the idea of bilateral free trade arrangement and explore the prospect for a land corridor between India and Thailand through Myanmar (Sharma, 2001: 14). During Prime Minister Taksin Shinawatra's brief visit to India in 2002, the Thai and Indian Prime Ministers discussed the proposed free trade area, the Asian Cooperation Dialogue, security cooperation, regional infrastructure, tourism and the ASEAN-India Summit. The two countries also signed an agreement on scientific, technical and environmental cooperation (*Bangkok Post*, February 2, 2002: 3). In 2002, Prime Minister Atal Behari Vajpayee made a brief visit to Thailand on the way back from the ASEAN Summit Meeting in Cambodia. Later, in 2003, he paid an official visit to Thailand. During this visit, the two countries signed a bilateral free trade agreement. In 2004, Prime Minister Manmohan Singh joined the BIMSTEC Summit Meeting in Bangkok. These exchanges of high level visits completely transformed the relationship between the two countries.

Ever since economic reforms and liberalization were launched in India, India has moved to the forefront of potential marketplaces and has been transformed into an opportunity for investment and trade. In addition, the relationship between India and ASEAN has also improved. Consequently, India was accepted as a Full Dialogue Partner of the ASEAN in 1995 (Gupta, 1997: 25). At the same period, Thai government also tried to open the new markets for Thai goods (Chongkittavorn, 1997: A4). Consequently, the "Look West" policy was formulated and implemented.

A concrete manifestation of Thailand's "Look West" policy was the Thai initiative for the establishment of a sub-regional economic cooperation grouping linking Southeast Asia and South Asia for the first time which was initially called BIST-EC (Bangladesh-India-Sri Lanka-Thailand Economic Cooperation) and later called BIMSTEC (Bay of Bengal Initiative for Multi-Sectoral Technical and Economic

Cooperation). This sub-regional economic cooperation was officially inaugurated in Bangkok in June, 1997. This brought together Bangladesh, India, Sri Lanka and Thailand (Gupta, 1997: 23-24). A few months later, Myanmar joined this group. In addition, Nepal and Bhutan also joined this sub-regional economic cooperation in 2003.

The main areas identified are cooperation in trade, investment, industry, transportation, infrastructure, science and technology, human resource development, energy, fisheries, agriculture, natural resources, and tourism. This economic cooperation has tremendous potential to bolster economic interaction between the emerging mega economies of South Asia and the booming economies of Southeast Asia. It helps in bringing ASEAN and SAARC closer and in deepening bilateral relations, particularly economic relations, between the member countries. A particularly important feature from the Indian point of view is the BISMTEC should help greatly in the economic development of the North Eastern States of India, which are geographically remote from the rest of India and have lagged behind in development despite considerable richness of resources (Gupta, 1997: 24).

The adjustment of the foreign policies in both countries positively affected economic relations. In 1991, there was virtually zero investment from Thailand into India. Between then and the end of 1996, Thailand had emerged as the tenth largest investor in India (Gupta, 1997: 26). During the past decade, there were investments in 110 projects from Thailand into India, but these account for only 0.01% compared with all of the foreign investments in India during the same period. For the investment in Thailand by Indian firms, 11 projects were approved by Board of Investment in 2004, and these accounted for 1.9 % compared with all of the foreign investments in Thailand during the same period (Ministry of Foreign Affairs, 2005).

Ties in the banking sector have been expanding. The Bharat Overseas Bank has been functioning in Thailand since 1947. The Siam Commercial Bank opened a branch in Mumbai in December 1995 and the Krungthai Bank also opened a branch in Mumbai in January 1997 (Gupta, 1997: 28).

India and Thailand have established several mechanisms and

institutional linkages to broaden, deepen and expand their economic relationship. In order to increase the trade volume between the two countries, a Joint Trade Committee was established in 1989. Since then, this committee has worked continuously. The last meeting was organized in September 2004 (Ministry of Foreign Affairs, 2005). In addition, a Joint Commission was set up in 1989. A Joint Business Council was established in 1990. A Cooperation Agreement has been signed between the Board of Investment of Thailand and the Foreign Investment Promotion Bureau of India (Gupta, 1997: 28).

In order to boost tourism in Thailand and India and cope with the demand of businessmen in both countries, airlines of both countries have recently increased their capacities and routes. It is expected that the Indian visitors to Thailand and Thai visitors to India either for travel or business will significantly increase in the near future. In addition, both countries are now promoting their interesting tourist destinations. The first car rally from India to several countries in Southeast Asia was organized in November 2004. Racers from 10 countries participated in a 20-day event which was flagged off from Guwahati, the main city of the Northeastern state of Assam (*Bankgkok Post*, November 22, 2004: 6). The promotion of interesting destinations for the Thai people by the officials of Andhra Pradesh in July 2005 was another good example of this move. Andhra Pradesh has focused marketing activities on Buddhist travellers from Thailand. In Andhra Pradesh, there are 144 Buddhism-related historical sites, most of them in the Nagarjunakonda and Amaravati towns. Amaravati, in particular, is a popular destination for Buddhists who want to pay homage to Lord Buddha's relics (*Bangkok Post*, July 1, 2005: B3).

An agreement on the twinning of Port Blair with Phuket for tourism purposes can be cited as another example of this trend. In June 2005, the city of Port Blair, the capital of Andaman and Nicobar islands and Phuket province signed a twinning agreement to promote relations through tourism, education, culture, urban development, commerce and investments (Sharma, 2005:10).

Bilateral trade, though limited in absolute terms, has continued to grow. Bilateral trade in 1996 was worth $ 895 million (Gupta, 1997: 27). Since then, bilateral trade has been on an upward curve. In 2004, bilateral trade was worth $ 2.04 billion (Ministry of Foreign Affairs, 2005).

A new era of economic cooperation between India and Thailand started in October, 2003 when the Indian leader, Atal Behari Vajpayee, paid an official visit to Thailand. On 9 October 2003, the Thai and Indian Prime Ministers signed a historic free trade agreement aimed at eliminating tariffs by 2010.

Prime Minister Thaksin Shinawatra believed that the agreement would give Thai businesses access to a market of more than one billion people. He also explained that trade was only one aspect of a broader framework, which included issues such as agricultural and biotechnology sharing, scientific and academic cooperation and visa and travel procedures (*Bangkok Post*, October 10, 2003: B1). The Indian Prime Minister Atal Bihari Vajpayee, in a special address to the Thai Parliament, said that he expected trade and tourism ties between the two countries to flourish. The Indian Prime Minister also said that the free trade agreement would offer huge opportunities for companies in both countries. Indian firms meanwhile would help expand Thailand's fledgling software industry, while Thai films were expected to gain opportunities in India's infrastructure, tourism and information technology sectors (*Bangkok Post*, October 10, 2003: B1).

For the role of the business sector, the Indian Prime Minster, during a luncheon of Thai business executives and their Indian counterparts on 10 October 2003, urged businesspeople of both countries to increase trade and investment. Prime Minister Atal Bihari Vajpayee said that while governments could help improve trade, sharp growth can only be achieved by businesses taking advantage of liberalization policies. He said that businesses from both sides could benefit from each other's needs. India can provide a huge domestic market and a low-cost, high-skill manufacturing base for Thai businesses, while Thailand's competence in infrastructure matches India's growing needs and India's software skills can support Thailand's rapid developing hardware capabilities (*Bangkok Post*, October 11, 2003: B1).

In order to speed up economic cooperation between Thailand and India, Prime Minister Thaksin Shinawatra made a one-day working visit to the Indian capital on 3 June 2005. He stressed, during a working lunch with a select group of Indian industrialists and business representatives, that the process of finalizing the free trade area agreement between Thailand and India should be speeded up. He suggested that the chambers of commerce and trade bodies from both countries should work out the list of items that can be included in the early harvest scheme which already has 82 items (*Bangkok Post*, June 5, 2005: 2).

Besides a meeting with industrialists, the Thai Prime Minister had a separate meeting with Ratan Tata, Chairman of the Tata group which has diversified interests ranging from steel to telecoms and automotive products (*Bangkok Post*, June 5, 2005: 2).

Since it was a working visit, there was no ceremonial reception and official banquet. Prime Minister Thaksin met the Indian Prime Minister, Manmohan Singh at his residence over dinner. Besides a review of bilateral, regional and international issues, the two leaders discussed security cooperation, trade and economic relations.

One concrete fallout of the visit was the signing of a Memorandum of Understanding on cooperation in the field of education. India's Minister for Human Resources Development Arjun Singh and Foreign Minister Kantathi Suphamongkon of Thailand signed the agreement in the presence of their two Prime Ministers (*Bangkok Post*, June 5, 2005: 2).

The Memorandum of Understanding was a broad framework under which to foster collaboration in the education sector. Institutions of the two countries would work out details later. Prime Minister Taksin is extremely interested in the cooperation between the two countries in education. In the Indian capital, he proposed that India open the education market in Thailand by setting up universities in that country. He praised India for its educational standards, particularly in the fields of engineering and Information Technology (*Bangkok Post*, June 5, 2005: 2). A few days later in Bangkok, he said that he was concerned about the quality of English teachers in Thailand and suggested that more teachers from India, Bhutan and Sri Lanka be invited to teach the language in Thai schools (*Bangkok Post*, June 8, 2005: 2). The Thai Prime Minister suggested that the Education

Ministry solve the shortage of qualified English teachers by employing teachers from South Asia to teach English and mathematics (*Bangkok Post*, June 8, 2005: 2).

While economic aspects have continued to dominate bilateral ties, a new form of cooperation in security areas has taken shape since the mid-1990s with far-reaching ramifications for the future of Thai-Indian friendship (Chongkittavorn, 1997: A4). During this period, the ASEAN gained more confidence in dealing with India. In early 1995, when India expressed a desire to join the ASEAN Regional Forum, ASEAN leaders responded positively and gave India a seat in the ARF during the fifth ASEAN Summit in Bangkok. The growth of the ASEAN-Indian relationship has in effect strengthened Thai-Indian relations, especially in the area of security cooperation (Chongkittavorn, 1997: A4).

Exchange visits by senior armed forces officials between the two countries, especially naval officers, have been conducted on a regular basis. Thailand also bought Indian-made ammunitions. It is interesting to note that Thai-Indian navel ties have benefited tremendously from the peace dividends of the post Cold War era. The absence of land-based threats has shifted the focus of the Thai armed forces towards possible sea-based threats and the protection of maritime resources. Frequent naval exchanges including port calls and training have increased the confidence of the Thai military toward India (Chongkittavorn, 1997: A4). In July 2003, the Supreme Commander General Surayud Chulanont went to India for a three-day visit (*Bangkok Post*, July 16, 2003: 4). The talks concentrated on improved cooperation, included talks on exchanges of military cadets, naval issues and the general situation in the region.

In order to build the institutional linkage between India and Thailand for security purposes, a Thailand-India Joint Working Group on Security was established. Meetings have already been organized thrice since its establishment, in May 2004, December 2004 and August 2005 (Ministry of Foreign Affairs, 2005).

Besides the traditional security issues, India and Thailand also recognize the threat of terrorism to global security and economic development and have agreed to cooperate closely to combat this threat.

Both countries have agreed to enhance collaboration against drug trafficking, money laundering, cyber economic crime and illegal migration, with a view to checking transnational terrorism and crime (Seetharam, 2005: B8).

At present, Indo-Thai relations are close and cordial in every aspect. Both countries which have been linked culturally for centuries, are now working endlessly to promote political and economic ties. If this century becomes a century of Asia, it is believed that Indo-Thai relations will also become significant part of the success.

Bibliography

Ayoob, Mohammed. *India and Southeast Asia: Indian Perceptions and Policies*. London: Routledge, 1990.

Chongkittavorn, Kavi. "Thai-Indo security ties enjoy peace dividend." *The Nation*. August 1, 1997: A4.

Ministry of Foreign Affairs, Kingdom of Thailand. *Republic of India*. (In Thai) http://www.mfa.go.th/web/479.php?id=125, August 31: 2005.

Gupta, Ranjit. "Indo-Thai Relations" presented at the seminar on "The Thai-Indian Relations in the Present Decade and Prospects for Cooperation in the Future," on 30 July 1997, at the Regent Hotel, Bangkok. The seminar was organized by the Faculty of Political Science, Thammasat University, the India Studies Centre, Thammasat University and the Information Department, Ministry of Foreign Affairs. The proceedings of the seminar were published in 1997 by the Faculty of Political Science, Thammasat University, the India Studies Centre, Thammasat University and the Information Department, Ministry of Foreign Affairs.

Jha, Ganganath. *Foreign Policy of Thailand*. New Delhi: Radiant Publishers,1979.

Kaul, Man Mohini. "ASEAN-India Relations during the Cold War." *India and ASEAN: The Politics of India's Look East Policy*. Edited by Frédéric Grare and Amitabh Mattoo. New Delhi: Centre de Sciences Humaines, 2001.

Majumdar, Asis Kumar. *South-East Asia in Indian Foreign Policy: A Study of India's Relations With South-East Asian Countries From 1962-82*. Calcutta: Naya Prokash, 1982.

Nibhatsukit, Warangkana. *The Relations Between Thailand and India 1950-1986*, (in Thai). Bangkok: Thesis, Graduate School, Chulalongkorn University, 1992.

Sardesai, D. R. *Indian Foreign Policy in Cambodia, Laos, and Vietnam, 1947-1964*. Berkeley and Los Angeles: University of California Press, 1968.

Seetharam, T. P. "Message from Charge d'Affaire a.i. of India." *Bangkok Post*. January 26, 2005: B8.

Sharma, Dinesh C. "India to study free trade with Thailand." *Bangkok Post*. November 30, 2001: 14.

Sharma, Dinesh C. "Phuket and the Indian connection." *Bangkok Post*. August 18, 2005:10.

The National Identity Board, Office of the Prime Minister, Kingdom of Thailand. *Thailand into the 2000's*. Bangkok: The National Identity Board, Office of the Prime Minister, Kingdom of Thailand, 2000.

Bangkok Post. February 2, 2002: 3.

———. July 16, 2003: 4.

———. October 10, 2003: B1.

———. October 11, 2003: B1.

———. November 22, 2004: 6.

———. June 5, 2005: 2.

———. June 8, 2005: 2.

———. July 1, 2005: B3.

Forty-Seven Indian Days in the Fifth Reign: The Genesis of Thai Modernity

SACHCHIDANAND SAHAI

❖

Considerable literature is available on the fifth reign, which examines various measures of reform that King Chulalongkorn took during his long rule (1868-1910). Most of the reforms can be traced back to his private schooling for about six years with a British governess Mrs. Leonowens and then with Dr. Chandler an American missionary until the end of his father's reign in 1868.[1]

No effort has been made so far to analyze the consequences of the forty-seven days which King Chulalongkorn spent in the British Indian territory from January 11 to February 26, 1872. I have elsewhere reconstituted the diary of the Siamese King for these forty-seven days, detailing the events, which took place during this period and gave a direction to the process of modernization in Siam.

Contemporary sources call the royal Siamese tour an "unprecedented journey."

In one of his dispatches dated December 16, 1871, the US Consul remarked:

> The king ... has embarked on this unprecedented journey – no other Siamese Potentate having ever

[1] David K. Wyatt. *The Politics of Reform in Thailand: Education in the Reign of King Chulanlongkorn*. New Haven: 1969, 30.

> ventured to leave his kingdom during his reign." The Consul further observed that the attendants of the King were all dressed in suit entirely unlike anything before known among them and behaved with singular propriety – altogether it is a very interesting and extraordinary affair. The old traditions of the kingdom are all opposed to any such movement.[2]

The Siamese King's stay in Calcutta from January 13 to January 22, 1872, was most eventful in more than one way. The young King came in direct contact with the British model of administration as practised in 1872 in the various departments of Government created by Lord Mayo, the Governor General of India. He was also exposed to the Asiatic Society, as the *Hindoo Patriot* (Jan. 22, 1872) reports for Monday January 15, 1872.

> His Majesty the King of Siam paid this day a visit to the Asiatic Society, accompanied by his private secretary, and Major Sladen. Mr. Anderson, the curator of the Indian Museum and the Assistant Secretary to the Society showed the royal party the rich collection of the Museum and rare and valuable Persian, Sanskrit and Pali manuscripts of the Society. His majesty was highly pleased to see some of the Buddhist works shown, and with the explanation given by the Assistant Secretary.[3]

---

[2] Despatches from US Consul in Bangkok: Despatch no. 56 dated US Consulate, Bangkok, December 16, 1871.

[3] *The Hindoo Patriot*, January 22, 1872, infra, p. 92. Major Sladen's Report mentions visit of Indian Museum as one of the day's programme. *The Hindoo Patriot* mentions a visit to both the Asiatic Society and the Museum. The present building of the Indian Museum was opened only in 1875, cf., *The Indian Museum: 1814-1914*, Calcutta, published in 1914. That the Indian Museum was housed at the Asiatic Society, 1 Park Street, for which the Indian Museum paid a rent, is clear from the contemporary proceedings of the Asian Society, W. Newman and Co.'s *Handbook to Calcutta* (p. 187). Published in 1875, this clearly states that the new building was not yet complete and that the Museum, in its old quarters, in Park Street, has enjoyed a wide popularity, the average number of visitors being nearly 700 daily, principally natives. So it is obvious that the King of Siam saw the Indian Museum collection at the 1 Park Street premises of the Asiatic Society.

At the Asiatic Society, Calcutta, the King came in contact with the work done by the Sir William Jones, who had founded the Society in 1784, and his successors. James Prinsep who deciphered the Pali inscriptions of Ashok was no longer alive. His researches of Ashokan inscriptions were available at the Asiatic Society and immortalized by the James Prinsep Memorial building on the bank of the Hooghly where King Chulalongkorn landed on January 13, 1872, and from where he departed back home. His early encounters with a growing consciousness for an Asian identity under the auspices of Asiatic Society made deep impressions on the King and helped him in later years to strike a balance between Asian traditions and a Western scientific approach. In the later years of his life he felt sincerely that it was quite feasible to maintain an Asian identity while adopting Western scientific modes of thinking.

In British India King Chulalongkorn had an opportunity to see the establishments of deposed Indian princes such as Wajid Ali Shah of Oudh and the Nawab of Murshidabad who were living in Calcutta after their kingdom had been annexed by the British. He also visited the two Maharajas at Benares – the Maharaja of Benares and the Maharaja of Vizianagaram. He witnessed all the symptoms of decaying Orientalism. While the traditional rulers – the Maharajas and the Nawabs – were clinging to Oriental pomp and show, the British were engaged in spreading railway networks, road links, mining and other enterprises to exploit India's resources. King Chulalongkorn had ample opportunity to realize the futility of oriental grandeur which led to the decay of existing structures of the social fabric. For survival as an independent nation, he had to choose between tradition and modernity. He opted for modernity in a massive way to cope with the mounting pressure of Western imperialism.

The King had an opportunity to assess the military power of the British in India and to understand the latest military techniques during his stay in Calcutta. He visited the Coosipore gun foundry and Fort William, the biggest arsenal of his times. The main reason for travelling from Calcutta directly to Delhi was to witness the concluding session of War Game or the Camp of Exercise, which was organized on the Prussian model. The royal presence at the War Game was a unique opportunity for the Siamese King to understand war tactics and to acquaint himself with the latest weaponry of the time. Throughout his career King Chulalongkorn remained interested in modernizing Siam militarily. It is true that Siam could not challenge the military power of the Western European nations, being herself a small one. But whatsoever her military strength, by modernizing it from a military point of view he had a rare opportunity to exercise his influence over the neighbouring Asiatic nations.

Taking the King of Siam and his royal party to the Camp of Exercise was high on the agenda of the British Indian government. This is what clearly emerges from the report of Major Sladen:

> It was one of the fortunate incidents attending the Siamese visit to India, that it occurred almost simultaneously with the assembling of the Camp of Exercise of Delhi.
>
> The season's operations were drawing to a close, and Delhi was therefore selected as the first city of importance in the interior to which the royal visitors were to be taken. The place was already well known to them, by the fame of its past history, as well as by the recollection of that memorable siege, in which it was recovered to our arms during the struggles of 1857.
>
> Added to its other enumerable interest, there was one which more than all other attracted Siamese curiosity, the fact that the visit of Delhi afforded an opportunity not only of seeing a large assemblage of British troops of all arms in the field, but also of witnessing tactics and war manoeuvers carried out in accordance with the practice of modern scientific appliances.[4]

In 1857, the Mutiny spread among Indian troops stationed at many cantonments in the great valley of the Ganges, Jumna and

[4] Major Sladen's report of the King of Siam's visit to India, file No. 53-57, Political – A, May 1872, Government of India (Foreign Department).

Gogra rivers. The Indian soldiers (sepoy), dissatisfied for various reasons, were joined by the Civilian population. At the moment of the Mutiny European troops numbered less than 40,000 in comparison with 230,000 Indian soldiers. And at this moment in the whole of India south and east of the Sutlej, there were only 11 Battalions of British infantry, the rest were either in Punjab or Burma or in the Crimean War.[5]

Though the Mutiny was completely crushed by the end of 1858, the British experience was so traumatic that they continued to analyze the nature and causes of the uprising of the Indian soldiers and civilians for the next twenty years.[6]

King Chulalongkorn visited India in 1872 at a time when the memories of the 1857 Mutiny were still fresh in the minds of the British rulers and native Indians. A number of British Mutiny veterans present in India came in close contact with the King. They must have shared their experiences and reminiscences with the royal Siamese guest.

One such Mutiny veteran was Major Sladen. He was appointed by the British Indian Government to attend upon King Chulalongkorn during the royal tour in India. He joined the King at Moulmein and remained with the royal Siamese party for over six weeks in January-February 1872.

That Major Sladen, the constant companion, attendant and guide of King Chulalongkorn did not resist the temptation of briefing the King about the happenings of 1857 is clear from his statements about the Mutiny sites in Delhi and Cawnpore, which the King visited with him.

Another Mutiny veteran was Lord Napier of Magdala, the Commander-in-Chief of the British Indian Army with whom the King interacted. He had served under General Sir James Outram who led the forces for the relief of Lucknow in the Mutiny of 1857. He participated in the second relief of Lucknow as well in November 1857. He was engaged in the actions of Mangalwar, Alambagh and

[5] Anthony Wood, *Nineteenth Century Britain, 1815-1914*, (2nd ed.), 1982, 226.

[6] Embree, Ainslie T., (ed.), *1857 in India, Mutiny or War of Independence*?, 1963.

Charbagh, in Lucknow. He had played a vital role in the capture of Tantia Tope, one of the key rebel leaders in the Mutiny. For his services in central India and the Mutiny, Napier had received the medal and three clasps. He had also received the thanks of the Parliament and of the British Indian Government and was made a KCB.[7]

During his stay in Calcutta King Chulalongkorn visited Barrackpore with Lord Mayo for a weekend on Saturday and Sunday, January 20-21, 1872.

In the course of twenty-four hours spent on the visit of Barrackpore the Siamese King and his British host Lord Mayo must have discussed matters of mutual interest. Those twenty-four hours were, however, sufficient for the King to assess the importance of Barrackpore in the military history of British Empire building – a cantonment for the native Indian troops under the command of the British officers since 1775. From this cantonment the native Indian troops were sent to Burma, Mauritius, Java, etc.

Barrackpore was the first scene in the Mutiny of 1857. On March 29 of that year it witnessed open defiance by Mangal Pandey, an Indian soldier of the 34th Bengal Native Infantry who attacked his British officers.

It appears, however, that the King did a much deeper study of Indian society, going beyond the limits of casual observation. By the time of the royal Siamese visit, India had been under British influence for over a century. Influenced by the liberal and rational views of the age of reform, the British administrators had already introduced a number of reforms in Indian society. With the impact of Western culture an intellectual class had emerged in Bengal, which was urging and supporting a number of desired reforms in Indian Society.

Raja Rammohan Roy (1772-1835) was one of the enlightened Indians who left his mark on Indian reform movement. In his own times, he had created a niche for himself in the international

---

[7] *The Dictionary of National Biography*, Oxford University Press, London, Vol. XIV, 75-83.

intellectual arena. Western radicals like Bentham and Roscoe greeted him and French savants honoured him as an equal ally. The fame of Rammohan Roy had certainly reached Siam before her King left for Calcutta in December 1871. In one of its issues, *The Siam Repository*, 1872: 124-25, published an exhaustive article on Rammohan Roy by Rajendra Lal Mitra: "The New Life in India" by a native of India who signs himself R. Mitra. It is not possible to ascertain whether the King saw that specific number of *The Siam Repository*. But the reform movement launched by Rammohan Roy had its followers amongst the Brahmo Samaj led by Debendranath Tagore and Keshabachandra Sen in Calcutta when the King visited the city.

Raja Rammohan Roy was the champion of a new education policy, pleading to teach useful western sciences in place of the classical lore of Sanskrit and Persian. After 1835, the state colleges confined to the teaching of Sanskrit, Arabic or Persian gave way to the foundation of new institutions for the teaching of European science, thought and culture through the English language.

During his stay in Calcutta, King Chulalongkorn must have been aware of a trend of ultra-radicalism famous under the name of Young Bengal, which dubbed Rammohan's radicalism as "coming as far as half way in religion and politics." The new movement sprang from the precincts of the Hindu College, which was established in 1817. The Bengali students of the Hindu College were quick to gain proficiency in the intricacies of the British political and legal system, the history of England, Greece and Rome and the European Classics. Exposure to European history had led these impressionable minds to respond to radical ideas current in the West at that epoch.

A Calcutta born Eurasian, Henri Louis Vivian Derozio (1809-31) was appointed a teacher in the Hindu College in May 1826, at the very young age of 17. He was very popular among his Bengali students, who were also in their teens. In 1827-28, under his patronage and often in his house, debates and discussions would take place on political issues. In 1829-30 Derozio and his pupils brought out a number of journals where they not only attacked Hindu orthodoxy, but also sometimes raised questions about the legitimacy of British colonization of India.[8]

In great alarm, the College authorities removed Derozio, the dangerous corrupter of the youth. On April 25, 1831 Derozio died of cholera before the end of that year.

Even after the death of Derozio, a band of his bright young pupils stirred contemporary society with their progressive ideas. This group was known collectively as the Derozians or Young Bengal.

Early in 1843 George Thompson, a well-known leader of the anti-slavery movement addressed several public meetings organized by the Derozians. Inspired by Thompson, the Young Bengal founded the Bengal British India Society on April 20, 1843, for the protection of legitimate rights of the subjects and open to all. In 1851, the Derozians linked up with other groups in the foundation of the British Indian Association. The Reverand Alexander Duff, a Scottish missionary who arrived in Calcutta in 1830, succeeded in persuading Derozio's pupils to accept "reformation as their models in place of the terrible issue of French illumination and reform in the last century."[9]

By their non-conformist behaviour – eating beef, drinking wine in public and taunting the image of Kali with the greeting "Good morning, Madam" – the Derozians scandalized the orthodox Hindus. But in the later phase, this insolent demonstrative gesture was followed by a pragmatic approach.

In 1848, one of the followers of the group wrote about "Young Bengal or the Hopes of India": "Young Bengal, liberal and magnanimous, is quite a distinct body from Young Bengal insolent and profligate. Young Bengal hard-reading had no affinity with Young Bengal hard-drinking."[10]

---

[8] Gautam Chattopadhyay, (ed.), *Bengal: Early Nineteenth Century* (Selected Documents) Calcutta, 1978, 32; cf. the Chapter titled "The Complexities of Young Bengal" in Sumit Sarkar's *A Critique of Colonial India*, 1985; Sumanta Banerjee, *The Parlour and the Street: Elite and Popular Culture in Nineteenth Century*, Calcutta, 1998, 47.

[9] Sumanta Banerjee, op. cit., p. 48.

[10] Soshee Chandra Dutta, *Essays on Miscellaneous Subjects 1848*, cited in *Renascent Bengal* (1817-1858), The Asiatic Society, Calcutta, 1st ed. 1972, rpt., p. 54.

In 1856, Kristodas Pal, an English-educated progressive, not belonging to the select band of Young Bengal published, "The Young Bengal Vindicated." In his judgement, "The Young Bengal is neither a wholesale condemner of Hindu manners and custom nor a sworn enemy to everything that is Hindu. He does not abuse the Brahmins for their misconduct or immorality or violently rushes against all that tallies not with his own doctrines.... The good of his country is the end and aim of his labour. He is never disrespectful or uncourteous. He is characterized by boldness and freedom. He is a hardworking man in the field of literature. He loves those habits and tastes of the English which are free from blame, but he abhors them that are the vices of an overgrown civilization and refinement."

In 1860, Keshabachandra Sen, a former student of the Hindu College published a tract entitled "Young Bengal. This is for you." It read: "Witness the improvement societies, friendly meetings, debating clubs, literary associations, etc., whose number is hourly increasing. Many and varied are the schemes proposed for the country's good but hardly do they pass the pales of theory. Social reforms are speculated upon but not practically undertaken..."[11]

Even in 1872, the legend of Young Bengal continued. Commenting on the strange distinctiveness of this group, Lal Bihari De wrote: "Young Bengal, with his fantastic and ever-varying dress, might have furnished them (the leaders of fashion in London), in his own person, parts of the national costumes of all countries of the world.[12]

Derozio, the leader of the Young Bengal had been lying in his grave for over forty years in the South Park Street Cemetery when the King of Siam visited Calcutta in 1872. The cemetery was not far away from 7 Wood Street where the King lived during his stay in Calcutta.

The King had not, however, to go to the cemetery of this Young Eurasian to learn about his doings. By now he was already a legendary figure as he had predicted in one of his poems before his death at the age of 22:

---

[11] *Renascent Bengal* (1817-1858), The Asiatic Society, Calcutta, pp. 70-73.

[12] *The Bengal Magazine*, Vol. I, August 1872-July 1873 cited in *Renascent Bengal*, p. 59.

And how you worship Truth's omnipotence,
What joyance rains upon me, when I see,
Fame, in the mirror of futurity
Weaving the chaplets you have yet to gain
And then I feel I have not lived in vain.

The surviving members of this group were all settled in their private lives, without any possibility of continuing the Young Bengal movement. But the path of protest and reform that they opened had made deep impact on the generation of the 1870s.

One surviving Derozian whom King Chulalongkorn must have met was Dakshinaranjan Mukherjee (1812-87).

In the first week of February 1872 the principal Talukdars of Oudh hosted an entertainment and a dinner for the King of Siam. Though the available archival sources do not mention the names of talukdars present on that occasion, it is almost certain that Dakshinaranjan Mukherjee was present as one the hosts in his capacity of he founder secretary of the Talukdar organization, the British Indian Association.

After the King's return from India, in March 1872, the political divisions at the royal Siamese court were clearly established. A contemporary observed that there were three political parties in Siam, now known as "Young Siam," "Conservative Siam" and "Old Siam." These parties, or more properly factions, may have corresponded with the parties of the King, the regent, and the old nobles.

The Young Siam unquestionably represented the King's party. The faction consisted of men (or boys) of the second Westernized generation in Siam. Most of their fathers were men who had sipped at the well of Western culture without great thirst, while their sons drank deeply. Most of them had at least partially Western education, particularly those members of the Royal family who had studied with Mrs. Leonowens or Dr. Chandler, and many of them came from families that continued to maintain close relations with the American missionaries.

The work of "Young Siam" gathered momentum only slowly. Its members were sufficiently strong by 1873 to be taking the lead in urging reforms of a radical nature. They began to issue their own newspaper. *The Darunowat* was published from July 1874 to June 1875 by one of the King's younger brother, Prince Phrom Woranurak. The newspaper published considerable foreign news and much comment on and discussion of reform that they felt needed to be undertaken in Siam. It was succeeded by the Nangsu "Court" Khan Ratchakan (September 1875-September 1876) published within the palace walls by eleven of the King's brothers.

The members of the group formed a "Young Siam Society" of which King Chulalongkorn's full brother, Prince Phanurangsi, was the President.[13] Incidentally Prince Phanurangsi had accompanied King Chulalongkorn on the royal tour to India, though he was a mere boy at that time.

Before visiting India, King Chulalongkorn had already initiated a programme of reform. A number of decrees were issued to bring reforms relating to the debt slavery, witness in litigation, court in Bangkok, records of taxation, sale of opium, etc.[14] These were important laws, but they were not too radical to upset the status quo or affect the fortunes of the nobility of the Kingdom.

After his return from India, at his second coronation on November 17, 1873, marking the end of the regency period, King Chulalongkorn announced his celebrated decree abolishing prostration in the royal presence. Sir Andrew Clarke describes the event in the following words: "… all the courtiers (were) kneeling or lying prostrate on the ground…. The King delivered an address, and at the end of it he announced the abolition of the practice at his court of kowtowing and lying down in the royal presence. As words passed his lips the recumbent figures rose, and the effect was described by those present as most impressive. To change a practice of abject servility into one of reasonable and dignified court etiquette was not a bad commencement for a reign of progress and reforms.[15]

---

[13] One of these brothers, Prince Phanurangsi republished the entire run of this newspaper in two volumes on the occasion of his birthday in 1923. Cf. David K. Wyatt, op. cit., pp. 44-45.

[14] Parachoom Chomchat, *Chulalongkorn the Great*, Tokyo, 1956, p. 50 ft.

[15] Sir Andrew Clarke, "My Fist Visit to Siam," *Contemporary Review*, Vol. 81 (Feb. 1902), p. 222.

It has been rightly suggested that the decrees that followed King Chlalongkorn's second coronation were more radical in nature, provoking open political conflict and opposition. The most important of these attempted to affect reforms in slavery, the judiciary, finance, and the political process, and the establishment of the Council of State and the Privy Council. Each of these reforms aroused some opposition and controversy and each of the major decrees had to be followed by supplementary expressions and explanations of the King's intention in promoting these reforms. With the establishment of the Councils, King Chulalongkorn's party "Young Siam" began to consolidate a position of power and challenge the old order.

The reform and their advocates, the "Young Siam" were attacked together. The most serious expression of opposition came in the "Front Palace Incident," which extended from December 1874 to February 1875 when the country came close to the point of political collapse and direct foreign intervention.

Though the crisis was settled in favour of King Chulalongkorn, it had serious consequences for the cause of reform and modernization.[16] The young King was forced to suspend the process of radical reform for ten to fifteen years in the face of entrenched opposition to them. Informing Sir Andrew Clarke about this, the King wrote: "I have felt it better to defer the prosecution of further plans of reforms until I shall find some demand for them among the leaders of my people. I have not relinquished them, but act according to my opportunities."[17]

Opportunities for reform came finally in the late 1880s when time took its toll on the old guards: the ex-Regent died in January 1883, and the second King, Wichaichan in August 1885; many of the officials and nobles of the regency period had also died or retired. With

---

[16] David K. Wyatt, op. cit., p. 61.

[17] Chulalongkorn to Clarke, 27 Nov. 1876, quoted in R. H. Vetch. *Life of Lt-General The Hon. Sir Andrew Clarke, London*. John Murray, 1905, p. 198, Cf., Xie Shunyu, Siam and the British, 1874-75 Sir Andrew and the Front Palace Crisis, Thammasat University Press, Bangkok, 1988, p. 59.

the help mainly of his brothers and loyal supporters, King Chulalongkorn embarked, once again, on a programme to modernize Siam.

In the meanwhile, after the passing over of the Front Palace incident, the King had to strive both to maintain the political détente established at that time and to live with it. His own party of young reformers, most prominent among who were his younger brothers, had to be asked to restrain their reforming zeal.[18]

King Chulalongkorn had grounding in British history and English language from his English teachers. He may have been familiar with the Young England and Young Ireland movements. But before launching the concept of Young Siam he had no opportunity to visit Europe. That he learnt about the "Young Bengal" during his visit to India is highly probable.

There are, however, obvious differences between the natures of the two movements. The boys of the Indian middle class represented Young Bengal. They did not have any power derived from the state or the state agency to implement their ideas of reform. They worked as a protest group against Hindu conservatism and as a pressure group for the British Indian government which took from time to time a reformist stance. In case of Young Siam, its exponents were the young King Chulalongkorn and his young followers. The King and his party represented a segment of political power, not powerful enough in the beginning to implement their reformist programme in the wake of opposition. They waited and gained time to carry out their reforms at an opportune moment.

The Young Bengal attacked the leaders of Hindu orthodoxy, who in turn opposed them vehemently. The Young Siam did not challenge the Buddhist social order. The reforms that they proposed affected the interest groups economically. So the opposition. It has been suggested that the Young Siam had internalized Western culture, accepting what was an addition to the Thai cultural tradition.

---

[18] Chulalongkorn to Prince Phanurangsi, 28 February 1875, printed in Natthawutthi, Somdet chaophraya, pp. 786-88 cited by David K. Wyatt, op. cit., p. 61, fn. 55.

Antagonism between Western culture and Thai civilization was resolved, if not at the earlier stage of Young Siam, at least in the later years of the King's experiments.

However, the first decisions about the adoption of the outwards of Western culture like dress evoked in the beginning a number of hesitations and considerations.

Dvaravati Cakras vis-à-vis the Deep Structure of Power in Indian Family of Southeast Asian Culture(s)

OM PRAKASH

❖

Cultural identity and distinctiveness emerge when people, with their inherent genius, deal with the given diversities of their own kind as well as of the social and natural environment together with different cultural influences received over various historical situations. The human agent, both individual and social, anonymous as well as biographical, conceptualized structures and articulate institutions. Endeavours in creativity and the necessary toils of life constitute the cultural personality of a people. The understanding of historical and anthropological influences cast by one culture over the other in their contacts of different kinds is unfortunately hidebound to theoretical and model-ridden approaches. As logical constructs of highly generalized and observed facts coupled with certain a priori notions, these approaches sometimes turn a participative venture into an invasive enterprise, innovative internalizations into model-bound imitation or imposition and anonymous social constructions of familial ties more or less on the lines of linguistic proliferation into the dichotomous breaks of Sanskritization, and/or localization, presence or absence, colonization or independent development from native roots in categorical terms and as a matter of historical or anthropological necessity. This paper seeks to look upon the interrelationship of Indian and Southeast Asian cultures as a familial extension and to illustrate the point by highlighting the significance of the Dvaravati *cakras* vis-à-vis the deep structure of power as embedded in the Indian extension of culture, in Southeast Asia.

The Shared and Inclusive Concept of *Cakra* and Power

The *Cakra* in the Indian cultural and linguistic tradition stands for a number of meanings.[1] Relevant to the present context among these is the meaning of sovereignty, which Monier Williams lists on the basis of the *Yajnavalkya smrti*[2] *and* the *Mahabharata*.[3] The *Amarakosa* mentions *rastra*, which may be regarded as equivalent to realm, kingdom or state and the *dambhantare* of the Medinikosa, which may treated as a word standing for the circle of religious followers other than one's own. The predictions made on Buddha's birth by astrologers as recorded in the biographical legends available to us, tell that the newly born child would either become a universal monarch or a leader of the following of a universal faith. Two kinds of universal sovereignties are thus posited in the Indian tradition, including both Brahmanical and Buddhist (Jain and other heretical traditions not excluded) and the notion of *cakra* symbolizes both. It may be pointed out that these two kinds of sovereignties, as they figure in the Indian tradition, are both as inclusive as well as exclusive Buddha's turning of *cakra* of *dharma* at Sarnath

---

[1] The, *Amarakosa* lists as the meaning of the word a bird called Cakravaka wheel of a chariot (*rathangam*) an army (*balam sainyam*) and also the political realm or the state (*rastrepi*). The *Medinikosa* adds *dambhantare,* a term of uncertain import, literally meaning a different pride but which may be construed to mean a religious Sect or belief system (*pasanda* as used in Ashoka's inscriptions) or order of heretical belief systems (also enumerated as *kapata, vyaja, chadma, upadhayahand kaitava* as interchangeable words for *dambha in* the *Amarakosa*) *as used in* later Sanskrit usage. It further adds potter's wheel (*kumbhakaropakarana*), a weapon (*astra*) and whirlpool (*jalavarta*). Monier Williams traces the meaning, wheel of a chariot to the *Rgveda,* discuss or weapon to the *Mahaharata* and adds further the senses of a military formation, cycle of the year or season, the plexuses of the body which the *Yogins* and the *Tantrikas* define in the context of *kundalini jagarana.* He also refers the composite word *dharmacakra* to Buddhists and Jains on the authority of the *Mahabharata.*

[2] 1.265

[3] I, xiii

symbolically marks the bringing down on earth the sovereignty of a universal faith before which people submitted drawn by an intrinsic necessity or conviction. The leader of the circle of political sovereignty of Buddhist conception similarly receives the voluntary submission of the rulers of all the four quarters because they all are convinced of the righteous conduct of the affairs of the universal state by that born leader, called a *cakravartin.* The Buddha thus turns the wheel of universal faith and receives the ungrudging submission of his innumerable followers and the *cakravartin* ruler turns the wheel of universal polity, which Monier Williams depicts through the wheel of a monarch's chariot rolling over his dominion and which the Buddhist tradition depicts as a celestial wheel guiding the course of the army of the Universal monarch out to receive the submission of the kings of all the quarters by dint of his unsurpassed piety and flawless conduct of the affairs of the state without the need to fight. Kings submit to him in the same manner in which the disciples and members of the laity submit to Buddha and the universal faith he preaches. At this level of high ideal there is no separation between the rule of Law or *dharma* and the rule of the Universal state or polity. The latter is enriched and made more attractive and upright by the presence in it of the essence of the former without which it is bound to be poorer and renegade.

Robert L. Brown is keen to suggest that the Dvaravati *cakras* "are not in a dialectic of power with the inscriptional texts" borne by them.[4] He prefaces this suggestion by some comments showing that the coming of gods, their forms, languages and texts to Southeast Asia alone was important, irrespective of the fact who brought them, for Southeast Asians were not interested in becoming Indians, or even mimicking the Indians. It was not important for them if the image of the Buddha was Indian, Dvaravati or Khmer. "What was important was that the image *was* the Buddha … There was no motivation for South East Asians to copy the various styles of Indian Buddha images. The motivation was to make images of the god that were meaningful."[5]

---

[4] Brown, Robert L., *The Dvaravati Wheels of the Law and the Indianization of South East Asia.* E. J. Brill, Leiden, 1996, 99.

[5] *Ibid.*

But the text appearing on the *cakras* are mostly from the Pali canonical texts like the *Vinayapitaka Mahavagga, Dahhmacakkapavattana Sutta, Dhammapada,* etc., and relate to citations of elements of four noble truths, links of causation, vision, understanding, light, and enlightenment of the Buddha. The entire discourse these short texts point to is a discourse of (religious) power to secure cessation of suffering. Importance of relic is yet to come to the fore at least in the texts on the *cakras,* though it is very much round the corner as revealed by the artistic triads of the *cakra,* the Buddha and the Stupa,[6] and the votive inscriptions recording donations of slaves and other things on the *dharmacakrastambhas* of Sab Champa and Lopburi bearing texts respectively in Sanskrit and Mon languages. Brown himself is in favour of characterizing these *dharmacakrastambhas* as "vehicles for secular statements," besides noting that "the votive inscriptions, with its careful listing of the names of the donated slaves, is a rare Dvaravati example of the kind of recordings we see frequently in Khmer votive inscriptions, listings that must have functioned as official community as well as religious, documents."[7] Surely, Dvaravati *cakras* are not a dialectic of power to the inscriptional texts on them if power is taken to denote the restricted sense of political power alone. But if power is taken to denote power in the broadest sense of the term the inscriptions on Dvaravati *cakras* make explicit what the symbolism of the *cakra* stands for in early Buddhism ranging from the aspects of power to understand and liberate oneself by securing the cessation of suffering for oneself contained in the first sermon of the Buddha to the aspects of the *bhavacakra* as visualized by Buddhaghosa or a little differently from the visual depiction of the same in Ajanta. On the *cakras* we have glimpses of the metaphysical concept of power differentiated in terms of endless and inevitable looking suffering and the *magga* or path of annihilation of it for oneself by human endeavour alone. The imagery of triads, that of the Buddha-on-the-monster, and the texts inscribed on the two *dharmacakrastambhas* referred to above, gradually and rather implicitly spell out the dialectical opposites of the metaphysical concept

[6] *Ibid*., 90-93.

[7] *Ibid*., 120.

of power quintessentially present in (not represented by) the *cakras*. While the first differentiates the power of human agency as the Buddha, of the Truth or Law as *cakra* and of the institution of the relic as the Stupa and that of the Sangha for the ministration of the Law as well as the relic, the second highlights the everlasting character of the metaphysical reality. The Buddha-on-the-monster endows the Buddha with supernatural or miraculous power and proclaims the superiority of this power over that of the monstrous power. The inscriptional texts on the pillars unfold the power of institution qua institution. The votive donations mark the awe and reverence into which the power of the political institution of kingship hold the power of the relic and the Law and also of the institution for their ministration, the Sangha, while demonstrating its power by endowing the latter slaves, animals and other material things of use.

The question is not whether the Southeast Asians were interested in becoming Indians or mimicking the Indians. The question is whether Indians ever wanted or compelled them to do so. There is no evidence that they ever exercised any colonial or even cultural and/or imperial hegemony over them. What they did was simply to furnish germs of parallel familial development in the same manner in which a mother language furnishes the germs for the developments of innumerable dialects equipped with the power to form a family of languages of their own. They simply provided the germ of their culture which Southeast Asians received on their own and developed them in the way they liked or historical circumstances permitted them to reproduce, innovate and rear. Queer indeed are the ways and powers of invasive models of interpretation. For several decades, Indus urbanism was supposed to have originated from ideas coming to the region flying on their wings from the west even though there was little in that quarter to compare with the Indus urbanism. The Rgvedic Aryans with no demonstrable material remains continued to be treated as mighty invaders of North-Western India for over a couple of centuries. Such impositions can never begin without the power to force or compel and die hard after once imposed even in the absence of the enforcing agency. Fortunately, there is no history of imposition by force between India and Southeast Asia in general and India and

Thailand in particular. Why then should there be such a keen consciousness to disavow what did not even happen. The spread of Indian culture in the Indian subcontinent too was not an outcome of forcible imposition. A social-scientific version of Brahmanical orthodoxy, Sanskritization is only a mode of interpretation that seeks to progressively misappropriate (and also from a retrospective effect) the achievements of autonomous coalescing of diverse social and cultural units for Brahmanical leadership. Fortunately, Sanskritization is also not at least historically there to distort the relationship between India and Southeast Asia. It cannot simply function without the *varn-jati* order, which is not there in Southeast Asia or Thailand. The very constitution of Indian culture to my mind is anonymous, eponymous and discursive in character. Without this essential character the phenomenal diversities of India through which it forges the thread of fundamental unity of deep cultural structure even across linguistic barriers would have been largely stamped out. There would not have been too many variations and regional differences in the literary and artistic creations even of a religious kind. It is pointless therefore to repudiate Indian-ness by showing the lack of model-bound-ness or non-source-oriented character of Southeast Asian cultural and artistic creations. Indian culture by its very nature was never suppressive of originality and autonomy of adaptations of its germs. The only ingredient of orthodoxy in it is essentially Vedic and Brahmanical and it is founded on two legal and intellectual fictions. The intellectual fiction is that all knowledge – past, present and future – is already there in the Vedas and the legal fiction is that all law – past, present and future – is already there in the Vedas. All heterodox systems in India have been fighting the outcome of these to fictions without the attacking their root. Fortunately, again this subtle orthodoxy too does not at least historically come in the way of Indo-Thai and Indo-Southeast Asian relations.

Power from Relic to Image

Describing how Buddhism might have localized in Thailand David K. Wyatt writes:

> For local believers (and would-be believers) in ancient Siam, Buddhism was a particularly attractive religious form that was based on the real life, work and teachings of an individual who lived many centuries ago in a place far away that they might have referred to as India, or as the Jambu Continent, but certainly nowhere close by. Their attraction to, and belief in, the Buddha and his teachings were made more "real" by creating a local physical presence of the Buddha. This was done in a number of ways: by planting sprigs from the tree under which the Buddha had attained Enlightenment, by discovering indentations in nearby rocks that came to be thought of as "footprints" which he had made eons earlier; by attributing to him prophecies that specifically foretold events peculiar to specific localities; and by possessing- and venerating physical relics of his body.[8]

Needless to say, such references abound in the *Chiang Mai Chronicle*. Dvaravati *dharmacakras* and *dharmacakrastambhas* too may be added to the list, though they do not probably find mention in the enumerations of the above text. In India, too, the Buddha as individual was first associated with the greatest attainment of Enlightenment after which he started preaching and founded the Sangha and then probably, in his lifetime rumour's about miracles performed by him and his prominent disciples started floating and formed the basis of numerous legendary accounts about them. After his passing away his relics were enshrined in ever proliferating numbers of Stupas (till it reached the proverbial mark of 84000 in the time, of Ashoka) and started being worshiped on account of the miraculous powers attributed to them. The Buddhist Sangha became the custodian of the Law as well as the relics and its associated monument, the Stupas. The efficacy of the relics was, however, a Pre-Buddhist belief not only in India but all other societies and is related to the extremely pervasive religious phenomenon going back to prehistoric times.

---

[8] Wyatt, David K., "Relics, Oaths and Politics in Thirteenth Century Siam" in the *Journal of Southeast Asian Studies*, 32 (1), Feb. 2001, 35.

Ancestor worship is also recognized in the Vedic-Brahmanic fold as *pitryana* (vehicle of the ancestors) as against *Devayana* (vehicle of the gods). *Pitryana* as an independent religious faith in the Vedic-Brahmanic traditions was superseded by the *sraddha* category of rituals. Denigrating what it calls *sarirapuja* prevalent among the *asuras,* one of the Upanisadas says that the *asuras* seek to conquer the world by decking the body of dead with the *bhiksa* (food items or perfumes or flowers) and raiment by way of decoration.[9] The condemnation of the *asuras* for not giving gifts and not offering sacrifices to gods shows that they were ancestor worshippers in their own traditional and non-Vedic way. The two schools of Buddhism, Hinayana and Mahayana popularly distinguished with reference to relic worship and the worship of the Buddha and the Bodhisattvas as gods fashioned in the form of images. These names of the Buddhist schools also resemble *pitryana* and *devayana*.

Against this background of the centrality and power of relics in Hinayana and also in Mahayana Buddhism (for even after the rise of Mahayana the importance of relics as articles of worship and reverence did not diminish), Wyatt's observation that "earlier sources do no seem to ascribe supernatural powers to the relics" and that the change of ascribing such powers to relics began "by the time relics began to be discussed in the texts of Southeast Asia"[10] seems wide off the mark. To quote Xinru Liu on the point, "The Buddhists paid great attention to funeral rights and commemorated the dead with stupas from every early times. *Sarir puja* (funeral ceremony) was performed by the Buddha and other monks. The cult of stupa and the related cult surrounding the corporeal remains of the Buddha were eesential for early monastic life.[11] Schopen argued that *saira puja* did not mean relic worship during the early stages of Buddhism but meant a funerary ceremony and that only later did this word indicate relic worship. He further points out that judging by other evidence, rules about stupa cult, i.e., relics worship very likely existed the Pali *vinaya* but were eliminated later

---

[9] *Chhandogya Upanisad*, VIII. 8.5.

[10] *Ibid*., 36.

[11] Liu, Xinru, *Silk and Religion*, Delhi, 1996, 31.

on.[12] About Pusyamitra sunga, a ruler of 2nd century BC, India, the *Divyavadana* records the legend that when he proceeded to destroy a *vihara*, Kukkutarama was frightened by the miraculous roar of a lion and, returned to Pataliputra without accomplishing the task.[13] This miracle is obviously the work of the relic kept in the *vihara*. Relics were very much the central feature of Buddhism at least for the laity and also foreign and native monks on pilgrimage and the kings, otherwise why would seven out of the eight Stupas in which the bodily remains of the Buddha were originally enshrined be opened by Ashoka and translated into as many as 84000 Stupas?[14] Why were the Stupas of Sanchi, Andher, Satadhara and Sonari in India found to enshrine the supposed relics of the Buddha and his disciples from the 2nd century BC to the 1st century BC?[15] Why did Kaniska fight with a middle Indian king to obtain the famous bowl of Buddha and enshrine it at the monastery at Purusapura?[16] Why did Hui-li remark that the successful transference of relics was possible only when they were willing to go?[17] I-Tsing also shows that the failure of Ming Yuan to steal the tooth of the Buddha from Sri Lanka (664-65) was due to the unwillingness of the relics to get translated.[18] Hiuen Tsang paid three gold coins to worship the perietal bone of the Buddha kept in the Nagarahara monastry by wrapping it up in a piece of silk thereby obtaining a rubbing of the powerful relic with the help of which one could predict one's future.[19] The following is the chart[20] of famous

---

[12] *Ibid.*, fn. 3 and 4.

[13] Chattopadhyaya, S., *Early History of Northern India*, Progressive Publishers, Calcutta, 1958, 12.

[14] Liu, Xinru, op. cit., 32.

[15] Ghosh, A., *An Encyclopaedia of Indian Archaeology*, Munshiram Manoharlal, Delhi, Vol. I, 270.

[16] Kuwayama, *Seichi, Kapishi Gandhar shi Kenkyu* (History of Kapisa and Gandhara), Kyoto University, Kyoto, 1990, 49.

[17] *Hui-li and Yen-Tsung, ta-s'u-en-ssu San-tsang-fa-shih Chuan* (Biography of Hiuen Tsang), eds. Sun Yu-t'ang and Hsieh Fang, Chung Hua-Shu-chu, Beijing, 1983.

[18] Liu, Xinru, op. cit., 47.

[19] *Ibid.*, 33.

[20] Based on the details given by Xinru Liu, op. cit., 32-36.

relic pilgrimage centres of North-Western and Northern India frequented by foreign pilgrim in the 5th-6th centuries AD:

Bhallika and also Trapusa	Bhallika enshrining a tooth, hair, nail and a broom of the Buddha	These were near Bactra in Afghanistan but named after Indian merchants Bhallika who along with Trpusa gave food to Buddha after Enlightenment.
Purusapura	Enshrining the bowl of the Buddha	It was obtained by Kaniska after a fight with a Middle Indian King. Fifth Century pilgrims Chih-meng, fayung, Hui-lan and Tao-yin visited and worshipped it.
Bamiyan	The Buddha's tooth and the tooth of the legendary king of thae Golden Wheel	
Nagarahar	Perietal bone of the Buddha, Hiuent Tsang also saw the Skull ofthe Buddha there.	Worsipped by Fa-hien during a state ceremony conducted by the king. Hiuen Tsang paid one gold coin to worship and three gold coin to be allowed to wrap it in silk to obtain a rubbing of it.
Kapisa	Perietal bone of the Buddha	Shifted from Nagarahar
Gandhara	100 Litres of relic ...	Hui-li 39
Kashmir	More than one litre of relics	Hui-li 43
Pataliputra	One litre of relics	Hui-li 64
Kannauj	Tooth of the Buddha	Enshrined by Harsa after obtaining it by force from the king of Kashmir

The pattern of development of the power of relics enshrined in the *viharas* and Stupas in Buddhism and the places having such monuments turning into centres of pilgrimage and trade in India and Southeast Asia, Sri Lanka and China were alike. This tendency aligned itself rather closely with trade and motivated the kings and polities to encourage it for material gain, arousal and consolidation of peoples' support and political and diplomatic advantages. Wyatt has rightly attributed the prosperity of the emerging polities following and also including Dvaravati beginnings to trade and popularity of Theravada Buddhism which must have been fired by the following. The scaling down (and consequent spread) of Buddhist eschatology from meditation and subtle doctrinal questions to wish fulfilling and redemptive rites and invocations, absorption of compatible elements from traditionally held local folkbeliefs, ancestor worship, and furnishing of relics and monuments and centres containing them as concrete articles of worship of the benevolent power. This power fulfills individual wishes, ends miseries in life and after-life and also ensures, enhances and protects the power and prosperity of realms of the rules who have a worshipful attitude to it. The chemistry of this change was in all probability responsible for the welcome originality, autonomy and innovative variations of literary, artistic and political use collectively called localization without severing the familial ties from and totally diluting the overall identity of the deep structure of the primary source of cultural inspiration.

The relic translation of the tremendous impact of the Buddha's personality on the on the minds of his disciples, which evoked the subjective feelings of the rapturous adoration transported the same across the limitations of time and space in the old mode of ancestor worship. This was done not only in case in Kanakamuni and Krukucchanda Buddhas preceding those that were built on the relies of the Buddha. But the question is what exactly did this kind of perpetuation denote? What is the deification or elevation to what may be called Pirhood or Sainthood under Sufi and Christian traditions? Or was it making the Buddha an incarnation of a perfect human being like Ram and Krishna of the Hindu tradition? But did Ram and Krishna ever have their Stupas under the Indian or prehistoric universal norm of ancestor worship? They were only *kathanayaks* (heroes of popular discourses) soon elevated to godhood or Godhood. The traditional Hindu or Brahmanical paradigm sought to appropriate the Buddha when the Puranas declared him an avatara or incarnation. Many scholars believe that prior to it the Buddha was already deified when simultaneously with it or slightly prior to the rise of Mahayana Buddha images took place in India. But Bhikshu Sangharakshita contends this position on the ground of incompatibility between the theistic notion of deification and the non-theistic character of Buddhism.[21] Describing the historical phenomenon of the emergence of image and image worship in Buddhism he writes,

> What really happened was that since Buddhists believed that the Buddha had realized the truth thereby becoming its embodiment and symbol, absolute Reality came to be interpreted concretely in terms of Buddhahood and its attributes, as well as abstractly in terms of *sunyata*, *tathata*, etc. At the same time the devotion with which the Buddha was worshipped was analogous to that which, in the theistic religions, is the prerogative of the Creator.[22]

The deification of a merely human individual thus ruled out the translation of the Buddha's physical remains as sacred and powerful relics signified the perpetuation of Buddhahood as the embodiment and symbol of the Truth, the absolute Reality realized by him. The image signified the perpetuation of the same all powerful Buddhahood not by worshipful preservation but by artistic creation, though even preservation was not without an artistic ingenuity expressed in the form of a Stupa. The *cakras,* including *cakrastambhas,* too are similar artistic creations attempting to concretize the same Truth or Buddhahood in the form of canonical imagery of the wheel of the Dhamma with all the autonomy of localization. They have been rightly characterized as a rhetoric of transcendence and presence, whose dynamics is connective, rather than agnostic.[23] In the light of what has been said above, there is little doubt that this characterization of the *cakars* is equally applicable to the artistic monuments enshrining the relics as well as to images captivating the Buddhahood not only in Thailand and India but anywhere else despite all their variations and innovations.

---

[21] Bhikshu Sangharakshita, "Buddhism," in *A Cultural History of India*, ed. A. L. Basham, Greenwood Press, Oxford, 1975, 84.

[22] *Ibid*.

[23] Brown, L., op. cit., 97.

Power Translated to the Realms of Society and Polity

In the matrix of the Indian family of things culture is not a dialectical opposite of nature. Therefore, there is no need of a counter power, like Reason, Science-based technology or Social Science to control the power of nature. By itself the motion of nature is supposed to be cyclic while that of history culture (i.e. history) thus conceived is incremental and progressive, as put by Hegel.[24] The State as the manifestation of reason (with a capital R) is necessarily efficient and society as more or less an instrument of Reason is manipulated indirectly by its "asocial sociability."[25]

This "efficient-instrument-mode" of understanding runs like a thread through not only Hegelian but also all the subsequent constructs of power in the West because it is embedded in the deep structure of the Western family of cultures. In the constructs of the Indian family of cultures however all power is held to be essential and inherent in the ultimate existentialist as well as metaphysical principal. Realized from the existentialist route it is Buddhahood and theologized from the metaphysical route it is godhood or Godhood. So far as the human attitude of devotion and adoration to symbol of the first or the deity-hood of the latter is concerned, it is analogous and often indistinguishable from each other.

The translation of power in the realms of society and polity again proceeds from two different routes. Society is linked to power through existential relations of different kinds. All social relations are essentially power relations too because power flows to society through existential relations which are absolutely essential. These relations are perceived in terms of pleasure and pain, justice and injustice, fulfillment and frustration, victory and defeat, bondage and freedom, hegemony and autonomy and so on, both individually and collectively. These dichotomies are addressed alike, both to worldly or otherworldly aspects of power as also to the metaphysical power of gods, to the existentially realized power of Buddhahood. Theism or atheism of the belief system hardly makes any difference here.

[24] Collingwood, R. G., *Idea of History*, Oxford University Prcss, 1961, 114.

[25] This has also been described as the cunning of reason. See *Ibid.*, 116.

Polities are not independent of society. They are not of the nature of a bolt from the blue. They are the product of the collective and communitarian concerns of societies at the existential level. Polities and societies are, therefore, similarly related to the ultimate source of power, which registers its presence as Buddhahood or as gods or God and also as spirits of ancestors, tree, jungles, rivers, etc. It is a lively world of powerful beings of a different order. Rituals and ceremonies induce their presence and support. Misconduct incurs their wrath. They help in the creations of visible authorities in human and institutional form. Buddha founded the Sangha after he realized Buddhahood. Dhamma and Buddhahood, which, as the symbol of Dhamma, preserve and proliferate it and are preserved and propagated by it, in turn. It is a semi-societal institution inasmuch as it is not based on one to one kinship and other sorts of ties generated by birth, instinctive and vegetative interaction of various kind that bring groups and societies into being. If the Sangha marks the semi-societal presence of existentially realized atheistic Dhamma and Buddhahood, the social and communitarian groups denote the existential presence of theologically conceived manifestation of the metphysical Principle. The relation of interdependence between the two renders the existence of the semi-societal Sangha possible. The existential and the metaphysical are thus not totally exclusive of each other and unite in the Middle Path shown by the Buddha and so are probably only in the "efficient instrument" construct of power. As observed by Ciffer Greetz in the context of the theatre State of Bali, "The king is an incarnation of the holy; the ceremony creates him; the state draws its force from the symbolic capacity t enchant. But this does not mean that the dignified and ceremonial serves the efficient. The king is not constructed in this way to awe and terrorise the gullible, as Hobbes would have it, or mystify them, as Marx would have it, or even to legitimate the realm, as Weber would have it. He is still at the still centre of the world. The ceremonial realms, as autonomous, neither illusion, nor lies, neither sleight of hand, nor make believe. They were what there was." This echoes the deep structure pronouncement in the Mahabharata:

Kalo va karanam rajnah raja va kalakaranam
eated te snsayoi ma'bhuta raja kalasya karanam.

Whether the time is the cause of the king or the king is the cause of time, you should never be in doubt regarding this question, for the king is, for sure, the cause of time.

This is, however, the ultimate point at which power under the Indian construct of it translates itself to social and political domains. It is more or less comparable to power emerging from the Passion/Reason dichotomy of Kant and Hegel where the cunning of reason makes passion its instrument to control individual and society without direct intervention. Reason as the exclusive embodiment of power, though Absolute, is not the same as the existential presence of power in the Indian construct of it, including also what is excluded as passion and therefore as irrational in the Western construct. In the former there is no dichotomy and therefore no instrumentality of the irrational at the existential level. This is what validates the sacral in the state here in the ultimate analysis.

But at the practical level of the organization and functioning of society and state there is much in common with the integration and working of power of these institutions under the Indian and Western constructs of power. Thus once the *cakras*, the *dharmacakrastambhas* and other products of art, the gold coins of the "Lord of Dvaravati," alphabet and a set of urban pattern with prosperity and influences from Indian and Sri Lankan trade welded Dvaravati into a Buddhist civilization, polities of Dhanyapura, Haripunjaya and Lopburi were soon to come and take up cudgels against Angkorian domination. Inscriptions, relics and artistic remains from Ban Map Makhan village and some other sites indicate how the emerging polity of Dhanyapura was using relics to further consolidate its positions. The largest inscription in Pali and Khmer dated AD 1169 shows how the ruler of Haripunjaya, Adityaraja extracted maximum concession by way of an absentia donation from the ruler of Lopburi who had become independent of Angkor in 1155 when he sent a mission to China as an independent power almost soon after end of Suryarman II's reign in Angkor. This king fought back three invasions of Kamboj and Lopburi so the big donation recorded in the Ban Map Makhan inscription by way of donations to the relics named as Kamarten Jagat Shri Dharamashoka of Dhayapura was obviously a reconciliatory move. The endowments included a gift of 2012 persons, 40 plates, 20 cheng of silver, 100 elephants, 100 horses, 100 bulls besides besides land for relic worship (the *dhatupujakhettam*). The edict granting these donations was issued by Maharajadhiraja Kurun Shri Dharamashoka and communicated by Maheshnati Shri Bhuvanaditya to be compiled with by the local ruler of Dhanayapura Kurun Sunat probably under the authority of the independent ruler of Haripunjaya through whom the grant was most probably routed and probably for wooing whose support against Angkor it was issued.

After the recovery of Angkor following its capture and sack by Champa under the usurper Jayavarman VII, a religious device was resorted to for ensuring the allegiance of the vassals as described by the Prah Khan inscription of 1191. Images of different gods, including twenty-three images Jayabuddhamahanta made in the facial and body likeness of the king, were set up by vassals in their capital and most probably their potable counterparts were to be brought to Ankor, the capital of the overlord for lustration ceremony every year in the month of March. Jayavarman VII had built highways in the direction of east, north and west along with spacious rest houses to facilitate the grand annual processions. An idea of the proportions of the vassals' donations on the occasion of this grand annual celebration can be had from the Prak Khan inscription. It mentions the gift of 8176 villages, 2,08,532 men, women and slaves of gods, 923 overseers, 6,6464 workers and 4,332 women, including 1,622 dancers. Six of the twenty-three places where Jayabuddhamahanatha's images were set up have been identified in western and eastern Siam.

Similarly one can invoke Chinese authority to show how another principality Chen li-fu maintained independence in defiance of the authority of imperial Angkor even during the rule of Jayavarman VII and sent as many as three embassies to China in 1200, 1202 and 1205 before succumbing to Agkorian domination in 1225. This polity is regarded as centring around Ratbory, Nakhon Chaisi or even Supbanburi. The Chinese sources testify to the fact that people were

Buddhist and highly literate. Their script was familiar to the Chinese and the languages of the court communication to China resemble that of the Malabari Indians. Their ruler is reported to have lived in a palace, used golden utensils and worn lavish silk and red gauzes. His court observed protocols and was full of officials of different variety. The state is said to have received regular supplies of red gauze and pottery from China and also developed a poetry of its own on the Chinese pattern. It also received ivory, rhinoceros horns, beeswax, lac and cardamom from India, Sri Lanka and local sources.

Such examples can be multiplied but the upshot of the matter is that in particular applications of power the Thai, South East Asian or Indian states resorted to the same sot of devices to consolidate their influence, or fire their strategies for aggression, rebellion or assertion of independence as any in the Western construct of power would have followed. The religious and existentialist concerns of the people might be conveniently manipulated to suit political ends. But big donations, religio-social and cultural ceremonials were also publicly conducted and observed annually on a grand scale to rehearse and recreate the presence of the ultimate power that benevolently rules over the heart and existentialist concerns of the people, and ambitions, prowess and luck of the kings alike. For such grand build-ups the invasive power constructs of the West have found different modes of grand mobilization of nation-wide militia, armed forces, uprisings in revolt or revolutions, bourgeois, radical, liberal or nationalist in the name of ideological deities like nationalism, Fascism, democracy and open society or even globalization with none too infrequent bloodbaths of sagging humanity both for and against the cause of justice. The zeal and confidence in deliverance, collective and individual, is not fired by donations small or lavish but by enormous expenditure on technologies of destruction that help not only to terrorize, mystify and legitimize and also strike unprecedented bargains in the worldwide trade of armament amidst vituperative and wholesale condemnation of war and violence.

Sanskrit: The Link Between India and Thailand

Satya Vrat Shastri

❖

One of the most ancient languages of the world, Sanskrit has a sizable presence in Thai. According to Dr. William J. Gedney, "words of Indic origin are about as common in spoken Thai as are words of Greek and Latin in spoken English." This is remarkable in view of the fact that Thai is structurally entirely different from Sanskrit. It is coupled with Chinese in view of the two vital characteristics that it shares with it, monosyllabism and tone-variation. How then could Thai come to acquire an enormous corpus of Sanskrit words is one of the biggest riddles of linguistic history. Whether Sanskrit entered Thailand through Pali which came with the introduction of Buddhism or independently is a matter of debate. Evidences are not lacking in Thai even of the influence of Sanskrit over Pali. One of the most interesting instances of this is the Thai word "pracaksa," direct perception. The Sanskrit form of this is "pratyaksa" and the Pali form "paccakkha." Now, if Thai pracaksa were derived from Pali paccakkha, its Sanskritization in Thai would have to be accepted, for the forms *pra* and *caksa* would not go well with Pali genius. Similarly, the appearance of *r* would not do in *akhra*, Sanskrit *agra*, *marga*, Sanskrit *marga* which in Pali is assimilated to the following sound: *agga*, *magga*. All this would lead us to the conclusion that Sanskrit was not always on the sidelines in Thailand, nor was it Pali's close follower. It is only the new coinages like *sawad-di* from Sanskrit *svasti*, a term for greeting in Thai, *thanakhan*, Sanskrit *dhanagara*, for Bank, *thoralekh* Sanskrit *duralekha* for telegram, *Prapa*, Sanskrit the same, for water works, *Sathani-Vitthayu*, Sanskrit *Vidyutsthana*, for Radio Station and host of words like these have a Sanskritic ring about them. It is a tribute to the Thai power of assimilation that they have been naturalized in it, given Thai pronunciation, Thai spelling and, occasionally, even Thai meaning, e.g. *karuna* in the sense of please. Before attempting a sampling of Sanskritic content in Thai it would be pertinent to draw attention to the fact that Sanskrit words when adopted and adapted by Thai undergo changes in pronunciation according to Thai phonology. This change goes with the position of the vocables in word, their occurrence initially, medially and finally. *a* in Thai is generally pronounced as *o* in line with the eastern characteristic common enough even in India but not so when it occurs initially. An interesting example when both these types occur is found in the word *anekprosong*, Sanskrit *anekaprasanga* used in Thai for many purposes where the *a* of *prasanga* is pronounced as *o* while that of *anek* is kept intact. *r* and *l* occurring at the end of a word are invariably changed to *n* in Thai, the word *rajakumar* is pronounced *rachkuman*, Khmer as *Khmen*, *Samara* for battle as *samon*, *ahara* for food as *ahan*, *mandira* for temple as *monthion*, *sakala* for whole as *sakon* and so on. All vowel-ending words in Thai are changed into consonant-ending ones. *g* is changed into *kh* in Thai as we have seen in the word *agra* which in Thai becomes *akhra*, *nakhon*, Sanskrit *nagra* for metropolis. The Thais have the *mahanakhon* which is Sanskrit *mahanagara*. *j* is changed to *ch*, *jaya* is *chaya*. Chaya, a city in the south of Thailand is the Sanskrit Jaya. So is *Chayabhum*, Sanskrit *Jayabhumi* if it occurs close to *r* it changes into *t*, Nakhon Si Thammarat, the name of a city in the South of Thailand which is Sanskrit Nagara Sri Dharmaraja. *Vajra* is *phet* in Thai; *t* occurring medially is changed to *d*: Sita Sidabut not initially. In the combination word *tonmai* for tree *ton* is Sanskrit *taru* which with the elision of the final *u* makes it monosyllabic in keeping with the Thai tendency, then turns the final *r* into *n* in keeping with the system and the pronunciation of *a* as *o* becomes *ton*. With the combination with *mai*, a typical Thai word originally meaning root, it means a tree. Interestingly, *mai* is added to another Sanskrit word *phala* too, *pholomai* which means just *phala*, fruit. *d* occurring initially is changed to *th*: Sanskrit *dvara thuan* in Thai *dh* becomes *th*. In *dharma thamma b* and *th* becomes *ph*. The name of the famous Indian market in Bangkok, Pharurat, is nothing but the Sanskrit Bahuratna. The word for wife in Thai is *phariya* which, as should be quite obvious, is the Sanskrit *bharya*. For conjunct consonants Thai follows the system of Anaptyxis. With the insertion of *i* in between *r* and *y*. Similarly husband in Thai is *sowami*, the Sanskrit *svami*. *Sthans* of Sanskrit is *sathan* in Thai. The word for embassy is *Sathan thoot*, the Sanskrit *Sthanadutaotr Duiasthana* of *Dutavasa*. It also means road or station, *Sathani Vithayu*, the Wireless Road, *Sathani Rod May*, Bus Stand, *Sathani Rod Fay*, the Railway Station. *Rod* is Sanskrit *ratha*. The name of a well-known road in Bangkok is Sukhumvit which is nothing but Sanskrit Suksmavithi, a small lane. This is the longest city road in the entire kingdom of Thailand stretching as far as over 70 kms. Still it is Suksmavithi, the small lane! It is interesting as to how old names persist even when their form has undergone radical change. It must have been a small lane initially. But even when it has stretched on and on, the old name continues with it. The Southeast Asian region in Thai is called Suvannabhum, Sanskrit Suvarnabhumi. The bee is called *phang* in Thai which is the Sanskrit *bhrnga*. The word for part or portion is *phak*, which is Sanskrit *bhaga*. The name of an island in the South of Thailand is Phuket which is Sanskrit Bhuksetra. The *v* of Sanskrit is *ph* in Thai, *vidhi* is *phithi*. The word for museum in Thai is *Phiphitliapha*, Sanskrit *Vividhabandha*, the *p* occurring medially is invariably changed to *b*. Sanskrit *puri* in Thai is *buri*: Thonduri, Prachinburi, Kanchanaburi, Phetburi. *Punya* is *bun* in Thai. The *s* occurring at the end of a word in invariably changed to *t*. The two prominent forms of Thai poetry are Lilit, Sankrit Lalita, the love poetry and the Nirat the poetry of pathos. *Nirat* is the Sanskrit *Niraasa*. For sky Thai has the word *akat* which is Sanskrit *akasa*. For aeroplane the word is *akatyan*, Sanskrit *akasayana*. The three sibilants of Sanskrit *s* are all reduced to *s*, the dental one, in Thai.

There are certain words that have maintained their Sanskrit form more or less, e.g., *pariman*, quantity, Sanskrit *parimana*, *praman*, approximately, Sanskrit *pramana*. The only minor change here is the dropping of the final *a* and the change of the cerebral *n* to *n*. *Vela* for time is pronounced as such in Thai. So is *nalika* for hour and *sukha* for lavatory, *lok* for world, *rup* for picture of photograph, *lekh* for writing and so on.

With a little appreciation of Thai phonology, it can be seen from the above, that a Sanskrit word can be chanced to Thai form and from its Thai form can be brought back to its original Sanskrit form.

There are certain words that have while maintaining their Sanskrit form more or less undergone some change in meaning or shades in meaning. Such words for instance are: *krpaya* as it may be called in Sanskrit, as against its Sanskrit sense of compassion or mercy; *prarthana*, desire as against its popular sense in Sanskrit of request, prayer; *sanjna* pronounced in Thai as *sanna*, promise as against its Sanskrit sense of consciousness or appellation and so on. Such words might have belonged originally to Sanskrit. At present they are a part of Thai vocabulary. Most Thais may be least conscious of the fact that the names they have such as Pridi (Priti), Hongskul (Hanisakula), Visudh (Visuddha), Vinaya, Mahanond (Mahananda), Syamananda, Chirayu, Valaya, Usa (Usha), Priya, Anong (Ananga), Galayani, (Kalyani) are all from Sanskrit. To them they are Thai names of which they are legitimately proud.

As with the names of the human beings, so with the names of the cities, towns, provinces and so on. Behind the crust of their phonetic variation their Sanskritic form peeps out. The following may be mentioned by way of illustration:

Thai	Sanskrit
Ayuthaya	Ayodhya
Buriram	Pariranya
Chanthaburi	Candrapuri
Chayanat	Jayanda
Chayaphum	Jalapuri
Kalasindhu	Kalasindhu
Kanchanaburi	Kancarapuri
Lopburi	Lavapuri
Nakhon Ratchasima	Nagararajasima
Nakhon Pathom	Nagaraprathama

Nakhon Si Thammarat	Nagarasridharmaraja
Nakhon Nayok	Nagaranayaka
Nakhon Sawan	Nagaranavarga
Nanthaburi	Nandapuri
Mahasarakham	Mahararagrama
Mukdahan	Muktahara
Phetchburi	Vajrapuri
Phitsnulok	Visnuloka
Prachinburi	Pracinapuri
Rajburi	Rajapuri
Sakon Nakhon	Sakalanagara
Samutprakan	Samudraprakara
Samitsonkram	Samudrasangrama
Simhaburi	Simhapuri
Sukhothai	Sukhodaya
Suratthani	Surastradhani
Surin	Surendra (Puri)
Sawankhalok	Svargaloka]
U Bon	Utpala
Udon Thani	Uttaradhani
Uttaradit	Uttaratirtha
Yasothorn	Yasodhara

For a country or a region the Thai word is *Prathet*, Sanskrit *Pradesa*. One of the regions of Thailand bordering Kampuchea is called Aranyaprathet, Sanskrit Arayapradesa. Thailand in thai is called Prathet Jnani.

The origin of the title Cakri of the present ruling dynasty of Thailand is quite interesting, nay revealing. Cakri is derived from the Sanskrit Cakra, an evidence again of Thai proceeding independently of Pali.

The subjects in the Thai kingdom are known as *pracha chon*, Sanskrit *prajajana*. The different parts of the country are called *phak*, Sanskrit *bhaga*. A province is known as *Canvat* of which *vat*, *vata*, is Sanskrit. The word for countyside is *chonnabod*, Sanskrit *janapada*. The field or farm is *Kaset*, Sanskrit *ksetra*, the seed sown is *phued*, Sanskrit *bija*. Agriculture is *kasetham*, Sanskrit *ksetrakarma*. As per the practice in Thailand the king himself ceremonially ploughs a small piece of land to initiate the sowing operation. The ceremony is called *phiti charot pra nankhan*, *vidhi langala*, the cermoney of handling the plough. The Civil service is called in Thailand *rajakan*, Sanskrit *rajakarya* and a civil servant *kha...rajakan*, *kha...rajakarya*. Municipal administration is called *thesaban*, Sanskrit *desapala* and one in charge of it is called *thesamontri*, Sanskrit *desamantri*. A minister in the central cabinet is called *rathamontri*, Sanskrit, *rastramantr*. The Prime Minsiter is called *nayok rathamontri* Sanskrit *nayaka rastramantri*. The Foreign minster is *rathamontri tan prathet*, *tang pradesa rastramantri*. The minister of the interior is *mahat thai*, Sanskrit *amha thai*. The Director of Education is *Siksadhikan*, Sanskrit *Siksadhikara*. The Director of Broadcasting is called *Adhibodi krom pracha samphan*, Sanskrit *Adhipati karma prajasambandha*. The Parliament is *Rathasabha*, Sanskrit *Rastrasabha* and the Cabinet is *Khan ratha montri*, *Gana rastramantri*. The Secretariat is called *Ledhikan khanarathamontri*, *Lekhadhikata ganarastramantri*.

The word for road in Thai is *thanon*, Sanskrit *sthana*, for a foot path, *padavithi*, Sanskrit the same, for station *sathani*, Sanskrit *sthana* (Bus Stand: *Sathani Rod May*, *Sthana Rathaxmy May*, Railway Station *Sthani Rod*, *Sathana Ray*, A hall is *sala*, Sankrit *sala*, a door is *thavan*, Sanskrit *davara*, an arch is *toro*, the Sanskrit *torana*, a palace *Prasad*, Sanskrit *prasada*, a pavilion *vedi*, the same as in Sanskrit.

The word for enemy in Thai is *satru* which is pure Sanskrit except for the dentalization of the papatal *s* which is common with Thai phonology where the palatal *s* and the cerebral *s* are invariably substituted by dental *s*, the example of the cerebral *s* being substituted by the dental *s* being *rasi*, Sanskrit *rsi*. The word for friend is *mit*, Sanskrit *mitra* or *sahay*, Sanskrit *sahaya* or the combination of the two, *mitsahay*, Sanskrit *mitrasahaysa*. Battle or war in Thai is *samon* which is Sanskrit *samara*. So is *samonphum*, battlefield from Sanskrit *samarabhumi*. The word for weapon in Thai is *avut* which is from the Sanskrit *ayudha*.

The names of a number of trees, plants and flowers in Thai are Sanskritic. Thus *Bakun* in Thai is Sanskrit *Bakula*, *Padum*, Sanskrit *Padma*, *Kokonadu*, Sanskrit *Komud*, Sanskrit *Kumuda*, *Phutsa*, Sanskrit *Badara*, *Mali*, Sanskrit *Malti* or *Mallika*, *Chomphu*, Sanskrit *Jambu*, *Tala*,

Sanskrit the same and so on. For fruit Thai has *phon* (*tamai*) of which *phon* is the Sanskrit *phala*. The fruit of an action is also called *phala* or *karmaphala* in Sanskrit. So is it in Thai: *phon lakam*, *phala-karma pr laram-phala*. The word for tree in Thai is *tonmai*. *Ton* is the Sanskrit *taru*.

The names of the months in Thai have a Sanskrit origin. But unlike in Sanskrit they are based on the names of the signs of the Zodiac or *Rasis*. Quite scientific, the Thais follow a definite system in the naming of the months: the names of the months, with thiry-one days end in the word *akhom*, Sanskrit *agama*; those with thirty days in *ayon*, Sanskrit *ayana* and the one, obviously February with less than thrity days ends in *phan*, Sanskrit *bandha*. The Thai names for the months, thus are:

Thai	**Sanskrit**	**English**
Mesayon	Mesayana	April
Phrsanphakhom	Vrsabhagama	May
Mithunayon	Mithunayana	June
Karakadakhom	karkatagana	July
Simhakhom	Simhagama	August
Kanyayon	kanyayana	September
Tulakhom	Tulagama	October
Phrscikayon	Vrscikayana	November
Dhanvakhom	Dhanvagama	December
Makarakhom	Makaragama	January
Kumphaphan	Kumbhabandha	February
Minakhom	Minagama	March

Besides these genreral names, some of the months may have in Thai some special names based on *Borne* special events, e.g. *Visakhabucha*, Sanskrit *Vidakhapuja* for the month Lord Buddha was born, received enlightenment and attained Nirvana. Similarly, the month when the Buddhist monks start the rainy-season prayers is called *A-sa-la-ha* in Thai or *A-sa-laha-bucha*; *Asadhapuja* in Sanskrit. For seasons, the Thais have the word *rdu*, Sanskrit *rtu*, for time *vela*, the same as in Sanskrit, watch *nadika*, Sanskrit *nadika*. No word in Thai is found for a particular season. It is in the name of the dish *Krayasat*, however that the name of the season *sarad*, autumn, peeps out. *Sat* is *sarad*.

The names of the days too have a Sanskritic origin. As against the Sanskrit practice of adding the word *vara* or *vasara* signifying day after the names of the planets, Thai has the word van (day) preceding them:

Thai	Sanskrit	English
Van-adit	Adityavara	Sunday
Van-can	Candravara	Monday
Van-ankhan	Mangalavara (Angaravara)	Tuesday
Van-phut	Budhavara	Wednesday
Van-phrhatsabody	Brhaspativara	Thursday
Van-suk	Sukravara	Friday
Van-sao	Sanivara	Saturday

While talking of the names of the days, it is interesting to note that Thais have a very peculiar word for calendar. It is *Pratidinam* which is pure Sanskrit.

The names of the quarters in Thai are all from Sanskrit. The intermediate space among quarters is identified in the Sanskritic tradition with some deity or the other like Rudra, Agni, etc. It is Thai. A chart is reproduced below giving the names of the quarters and their intermediate points in Thai with their Sanskrit originals and English equivalents to help form a clear idea of the influence that Sanskrit has exercized:

Udorn
Uttara
North

Phayap
Vayavya
North West

Isan
Isana
North East

Hawradi
Nairrti
South West

Akhane
Agneya
South East

Thaksin
Daksina
South

Thai has words for all the four *Varnas*, castes, which are the same as in Sanskrit except for certain phonetic variations and semantic peculiarities. *Brahmana* is called *Phram*, *Ksatriya Kasat*, *Vaisya Phait* and *Sudra Sud* in Thai. Of these *Phait* and *Sud* are of academic interest only, being no longer in use in popular speech. The word for merchant current in popular Speech is *Vanit* which is a changed form of Sanskrit *Vanij* and is more often than not pronounced as *Phanit* or *Phanij*. Apiece with it is Thai *Kasat* from the Sanskrit *Ksatriya*. The King is styled *Mahakast*, *Mahaksatriya*. It could be that *kasat* is a derivative of *ksatra* and not *ksatriya* which word is also part of Sanskrit vocabulary.

The concept of the four stages, *Asraas*, in the life of a person is not altogether unknown to Thailand where words for at least two stages, *Brahmacarya* and *Grhastha*, do exist. *Brahmacarya* is called *phrommacan* which means abstienence from sex. It is not often used with the word *praphrt*, Sanskrit *pravrtti*, practice: *Praphrt Phrommaehan*, practice of Brahmacarya. *Grhastha* is called *Grhat*, a householder. There are no words for *Vanaprastha* and *Sannyasa* in Thai.

There are words for three samskaras or religious rites, in Thai. They are: *Namakorn*, Sanskrit *Namakarana*, naming or Christening *Vivaha*, *Vivahamonkhon* and *Monkhon Smrot*, Sanskrit *Vivaha*, *Vivahamange Mangalasamarasa* for marriage and *Jhapanakicca*. Sanskrit *Kaspanakrtva* (*Antyesti*) is for last rites, the funeral.

The common word for a deity is *thevada*, Sanskrit *devata*. The male one is called *theva*, Sanskrit *deva* and the female one *thevi*, Sanskrit *devi*. The Hindu gods known in Thailand which have words for them in thai are Phram, Sanskrit Brahma, Narai or Phitsanu, Sanskrit Narayana and Visnu respectively, Isuan, Sanskrit Ganesa, Laksami, Sanskrit Laksmi, Sida, Sanskrit Sita and Saraswadi, Sanskrit Sarasvati.

Along with gods and goddesses of the Hindu pantheon there are words in Thai for the spiritual and the holy people like *rasi*, Sanskrit *rsi*, noticed earlier in the context of the dentalization of the celebral, *muni*, the same in Sanskrit and *daba*, Sanskrit *tapasa*.

Now a word about the different sciences and disciplines. It is interesting to know as to how they are called in Thai:

English	Thai	Sanskrit original
Anthropology	Mansugyavidya	Manusyavidya
Economic	Sethsat	Sresthasatra
Logic	Takavidya	Tarkavidya
Psychology	Cittavidya	Cittavidya
Ethics	Cariyasat	Caryasastra
Humanities	manusasat	manusyasastra
Sociology	Sankhom vidya	Sangamavidya
Linguistics	Bhasasat	Bhasasastra
History	Pravattisat	Pravrttisastra
Political Science	Rathasat	Rastrasastra
Mathematics	Khanitsat	Ganitasastra
Philosophy	Prajna	Prajna
Zoclogy	Sattvavidya	Sattvavidya
Biology	Jivavidya	Jivavidya
Science of Teaching	Kharusat; Siksasat	Gurusastra, Sikasast
Law	Nitisat	Nitisastra
Ethnology	Chativandvidva	jativarnavidya
Engineering	Vissavakammasat	Visvakarmasastra
Medicine	Phaityasat	Vaidyasastra
Surgery	Sallayasat	Salyasastra
Pathology	Ayursat	Ayuhsastra

As may be seen a particular order is noticeable in the nomenclature. The words which in English end in logy are rendered in Thai by the *tervidya*, while those ending in ics by *sat*, Sanskrit *Sastra*.

The institutions of higher learning in Thailand have Sanskrit names. The Colleges are called *Vidyalayas* and the Universities *Mahavidyalayas*, the words being pronounced as *Vitthayalaya* and *Mahavitthayalaya* respectively. For school, however, a typical Thai word *Rong Rien* is used. But when it comes to denoting a Primary or Secondary School, the words *Prathom*, Sanskrit *Prathama* and *Mathbhayom*, Sanskrti *Madhyama* are prepositioned. Simiarly prepositioned to the same, *Rong Rien*, are the words *Anuban*, Sanskrit *Anupala* and *Achip*, Sanskrit *Ajiva* to denote the Motessary school and the vocational School respectively.

The words for some of the University officials are Sanskritic in origin. The Dean is called *khanabody*, Sanskrit *Ganapati*, the President (vice-chancellor) of the University is *Adhikanbody*, Sanskrit *Adhikarapati*. The Ministry of Education is called *Kasuang Siksadhikan*, *Kasuang Siksadhikara*.

The terms for the various University degrees in Thailand are also typically Sanskritic. The Bachelor's degree is called *Bandit*, Sanskrit *Pandita* and the Master's degree *mahapandit*, Sanskrit *Mahapandita*. For the reseach degree, the Ph.D the word is *Dussadi Bandit*, Sanskrit *Tusti Pandita*. For research, the Thai word is *vichai*, Sanskrit *vicaya*, gathering or collecting. At least three Universities in Thailand have Sanrkritic names the Universities of Dhammasat, Sanskrit Dharmasastra, Silpakorn, Sanskrit *silpakara* and *kasersat*, Sanskrit *Ksetrasastra*.

Before the discussion on the Sanskrit content in Thai is brought to a close, it may be pertinent to make a reference to the evolution of a phenomenon in Thai of combination words which assumes three forms:

- Where two Sanskrit words meaning the same are joined together to convey the same sense like *mitsahay* in the sense of a friend where two Sanskrit words *mitra* and *sahaya* are coalesced.
- Where two words, one Sanskrit and the Thai, both meaning the same are joined together like *rangkay*, meaning body, *rang* of Thai meaning body and *kaya* of Sanskrit also meaning body are combined, the combination giving the sense of the body.
- Where two words, one of Sanskrit and the other of Thai, each carrying its own sense, are combined e.g. *bangrak*, the name of a locality in Bangkok where *bang* of Thai means place and *rak* which is Sanskrit *raga* means love; the words meaning the place of love, considered auspicious for the newly-weds. The Thai name for Bangkok is Krungthev; Bangkok is an international name; no Thai would ever use it – where *krung* of Thai means place and they, Sanskrit *deva* means god, the whole word Bangkok meaning the place of gods. The Thais are very proud of their capital city which for them is the city of gods and their country *udomthani*, the best place, Sanskrit *uttamasthani*: Another interesting Thai-

Sanskrit combination word is *namtan* meaning sugar where *nam* of Thai means water or juice or extract and is combined with *tan*, Sanskrit *tala* meaning palm. This is indicative of the fact that originally palm *gur* obtained from palm juice or extract was the sweetening agent for the Thais. Even if it is no longer so, the name still persists.

Cultural Linkages of Thailand and India with Special Reference to Kathak and Thai Classical Dance

MANDAVI SINGH

India is very rich with a variety of highly established art forms. In the field of classical dance we have a number of forms like Kathak, Bharatnatyam, Odissi, Manipuri, Kathakali, Kuchipudi and Mohiniattam. Each dance form has a separate identity with a unique style and traditional background.

Kathak is the classical dance of north India. The name Kathak is linked with "story telling." The one who tells the story is called the Kathak, that is the storyteller. While performing, the storyteller used to sing, dance and narrate different stories mainly from the Mahabharat and the Ramayana. This art had its roots in religion and was handed down from generation to generation as an oral tradition.

Though Kathak had a strong religious base, there was a remarkable change in the content and presentation during the medieval period, due to the influence of the Mughal rulers, who patronized Indian music and dance. Kathak acquired a different character shifting from its religion oriented aspect to the form of entertainment. Kathak flourished during the period of last Nawab of Lucknow – Wajid Ali Shah.

The two major aspects of Kathak are *Nritta* and *Abhinaya*. *Nritta* is a pure dance with two basic ingredients, the *Tala* and the *Laya*. The

Tala means a time cycle while the *Laya* denotes speed and tempo. *Nritta* is not a dance of expression. In *Nritta* the dancer performs a variety of rhythm patterns expressed through footwork which is known as *Tatkar*.

The other important aspect of Kathak, *Abhinaya* implies the rendering of the meaning of a song or a story through effective facial expressions, different gestures of the hand and body posture.

The golden era of Thai dance was during the reign of King Boramakot in the Ayutthaya Period and King Rama II in the Rattanakosin period. There was a great influence of western civilization and culture on Thai Classical Dance Drama during the period of King Rama VI (also known as King Vajirvudh) who wrote, produced and directed plays. Modern dance drama, the Lakhon Phu, (spoken drama) and the Lakhon Rong, (song drama) was introduced as a way to prepare the Thai people for the modem world.

Thai dancers hold their bodies upright from the neck to the hips, moving up and down using only their knees, and stretching to the rhythm of the music. The arms and hands in Thai dancing are held in curves at different levels but do not point like in a ballet. The beauty of the dancers depends on how well these curves and angles are maintained in relation and proportion to the whole body.

The actors mime the storyline and lyrics provided by a singer and chorus offstage. Traditionally, there are 108 basic movements, which are different for men and women. In order to perform well in the dance drama, dancers have to learn the language of gestures. Although there are strict patterns of movements to follow, dancers can still explore their individual talents as creative artists.

Thai drama was usually performed for royal entertainment and special occasions like birthdays, welcome ceremonies, etc. Among various types of drama the Khon, the Lakhon and the Hun were the prominent forms but nowadays many of the older forms have disappeared.

The Khon, a famous masked dance drama, is performed by dancers wearing brilliantly crafted masks. Normally, the Khon performances are taken from different episodes in the Ramakian. The formal movements of the Khon performances make the acting and dancing inseparable. The Lakhon, a graceful and beautiful dance drama is less formal than the Khon. Lakhon dancers do not wear masks but instead don the *chada*, the jewelled crown headdress.

Thailand and India have many similarities especially in the field of dance, language and religion. We find that the Khon dance from Thailand has some similarities to the Kathakali dance form of South India. Khon is a mask dance and generally performed by men. The female characters are performed by women while in Kathakali both the characters of male and female performed by man. The theme of both these dance forms are taken from the Puranas. But the stories in the Khon dance are taken from the Ramayana. Previously, women characters of both the dances were performed by men but nowadays women have also started performing as female characters.

In Thailand, the Ramayana is known as the Ramakian and the stories in the Khon dance are only from the Ramayana, while in India, Krishna has a major role in most dance themes.

The Kathak and the Lakhon dance forms have many similarities. Both these dance forms developed and flourished in the court of Kings. The Lakhon is purely an entertainment-oriented dance form presented in the court with its themes of love, hero worship, army and fight sequences, etc. Some kings also wrote stories from this dance form. Kathak, however, was originally based on religious themes, later it was made more attractive with entertainment aspects involving the themes of the Sringar *rasa*, which were presented in the courts of kings. Another aspect of the Kathak are the compositions which were composed by some kings like the Nawab Wajid Ali Shah and Raja Chakradhar Singh, and others.

The Lakhon dance performances are based on stories of certain themes performed with music and songs. To express the story, the dancers use words as well as body language. Music and songs are provided by the accompanying artists. The hand gestures are fixed and the movement of the hands to express a particular portion by a particular hand is also fixed. Another important aspect, of the facial expression, has not been given much importance while footwork is incorporated only to balance the body, not to show any technical aspect of the dance.

In Kathak as well the music and songs are provided by the accompanying artists. The performer shows the expression only through different *bhavas* (that is the expression of the face). The performer also performs only the rhythm patterns which is known as the *bol* with the footwork showing complicated technicalities of rhythm, a major aspect of Kathak. The performer should have perfect control over the rhythm to perform such footwork.

Just like in the Lakhon dance, Kathak also has hand and body gestures to express certain feelings. In the Lakhon dance, however, the hand gestures do not have any particular names, while the names for the body gestures are prescribed. In Kathak, the name for hand gestures are fixed but no name have been prescribed for body gestures.

The music for Thai classical dance is provided with instruments like the Drum, Ranad, Saw (similar to the Sarangi), Ching (similar to the Manjira) and Clap. Both men and women sing songs. Similarly, in Kathak, both men and women perform the songs and the instruments used are the Tabla, Harmonium, Sarangi, Sitar, etc.

From these above pointers we understand that there is a very strong link between the two countries, that Thailand and India have many similarities. I have simply thrown light on the dance forms of these two countries, but if we go deeper we can find the same reflections in the field of religion, culture, language and other various aspects of day-to-day life.

Thailand as a Bridge Between India and ASEAN

PRADEEP K. KAPUR

❖

Known as Siam until 1939, Thailand is the only South East Asian country which was never subjected to a western colonial power. Her status as an independent nation of Asia throughout the colonial era, has offered her a great deal of advantage, from the point of view regional cooperation in modern times.

Physical Routes of Regional Cooperation: Sea Route, Land Route, Air Route

In ancient times, regional cooperation and contact were established through land route and sea route. There is considerable research material on sea routes between India and South East Asia in general and Thailand in particular. We know about some of the flourishing ports in both the regions, which played an active role in early contact between the two regions.

However, knowledge of land route in ancient times has remained inadequate, in spite of great strides made in researches on South East Asia, though it is generally agreed that the land route was as important as the sea route. Nor is the knowledge and data on the present state of land routes between India and the countries of South East Asia adequate. Only recently, in 2004, a good beginning was made to obtain the latest data on the present state of the land route between these two regions. I am referring to the India-ASEAN Car Rally held in 2004. But, before coming to this important event, I would like to discuss in brief the background of India-ASEAN interaction, since Thailand is a major role player in ASEAN and Thailand could play an important role in expanding India's relationship with this regional apex body.

Myanmar acts as some sort of buffer state between India and the remaining nine states of the ASEAN. After crossing this buffer zone by land route, we enter Thailand, which is the veritable gateway to the ASEAN countries, as far as India is concerned. The whole of peninsular South East Asia – Lao, Cambodia, Vietnam, Myanmar and Singapore – can be reached by roads through Thailand. One of the biggest advantages of Thailand is that its road and rail links are excellent, which take us in the fastest possible way to the Lao, Cambodia and the Malay borders. It may perhaps be useful for India to consider taking some initiatives to assist in the internal road links in Lao, Myanmar and Cambodia, where already a number of international agencies are working to support the local governments to build new roads and create transport infrastructure in the countries bordering Thailand.

Through the southern corridor of Thailand, which consists of a land strip of 50 kilometres at some places, we reach up to Singapore and from there, airborne or sea-borne journeys to Indonesia or Philippines are possible. In the modern context, though direct air connections do exist in certain cases between India and the South East Asian countries, both Thailand and Singapore offer excellent connections as regional hubs.

Genesis of India and ASEAN Interaction

Since the inception of the ASEAN in the 1960s, India has constantly watched the progress of this regional organization with deep interest and a sense of solidarity. In successive phases, first as a sectoral dialogue partner, then as a full dialogue partner, and, thereafter, as a member of the ASEAN Regional Forum (ARF), India has been participating in the process of wider regional cooperation. It attained the status of Summit Partner of ASEAN at the level of Heads of State/Heads of Government in November 2002. Its status as a Summit Partner implies more active and extensive programmes of cooperation with the region. The role and importance of Thailand has immensely increased in this changed scenario. Thailand enjoys the neighbourhood of four ASEAN countries – Myanmar, Cambodia, Lao PDR, and Malaysia, sharing respectively 1800, 803, 1754 and 506 kms of border. Its unique position vis-à-vis the ASEAN nations of mainland and insular South East Asia, renders it much more important for India. As a Summit Partner of the ASEAN, closer social, economic and cultural relations have to be designed and developed for the integration of India in the broader regional framework of the ASEAN.

The Launch of the Open Skies Policy by the Government of India

During the First India-ASEAN Summit Meeting in Phnom Penh, Cambodia, in November 2002, the Prime Minister of India announced the Open Skies Policy. It was perhaps for the first time in the aviation history of India that such a liberal step was taken, specifically in the context of the regional grouping of the ASEAN countries. A total of twenty-two airports were offered for direct flight connections with the ASEAN countries.

As a result of the Open Skies Policy, more and more airlines, both from the public and the private sector, are now flying to newer destinations both in India and in ASEAN, and expanding their areas of operations. This is resulting in facilitating travel by making it less expensive and offering a wider choice of airlines and destinations.

The India-ASEAN Car Rally

The geo-political importance of Thailand for India in the context of the ASEAN became obvious on the eve of the 1st India-ASEAN Car Rally, which was organized in November-December 2004 by the Government of India in collaboration with the other Governments of the ASEAN countries and the Confederation of India Industry (CIl) as the main sponsor.

The Federation of the Motor Sports Club of India planned and executed the rally on behalf of the sponsors.

This was indeed a landmark event. It was for the first time in history, that the people from the different countries of this region travelled together as one group, by cars, and traversed more than eight thousand kilometres from India to eight ASEAN countries in about three weeks. The rally was flagged off from Guwahati in the North-east India by the Indian Prime Minister. After the rally had crossed Myanmar and Thailand, the leaders of ASEAN and India jointly flagged it off from Vientiane, Lao PDR, where the India-ASEAN Summit was being held. It then moved through Vietnam, Cambodia, Malaysia and Singapore before concluding in Indonesia.

In many countries, the participants of the rally were welcomed as ambassadors and envoys would have been welcomed in the ancient times.

On that occasion, I happened to be present in Phnom Penh as Ambassador of India to Cambodia. I was, therefore, able to contribute some ideas, which helped in giving shape to the Car Rally in different aspects. From Phnom Penh, I could realize the importance of Thailand as a key to India's overture to ASEAN.

Thailand was the only country, which had to be crossed twice by the Car Rally. On their journey from India and Myanmar to Lao PDR, the rally went through northern Thailand. Thereafter, on the way from Cambodia to Malaysia, it again had to traverse through southern Thailand. Therefore, for India, Thailand is a land-bridge with the Indo-China countries of Cambodia, Lao PDR, and Vietnam, and also for the other ASEAN countries, including Malaysia, Singapore, and from there on to Brunei and Indonesia.

It was hardly noticed and it is still rarely realized that it is through Thailand as a real bridge that India could get access to so many countries of the ASEAN through the land route.

The Present Status of the Land Route

Currently, the land routes between India and Myanmar are being developed. At present, the Tamu-More border crossing is functional. Long-term plans are being evolved for rail connectivity to be established between India and the ASEAN countries through Myanmar and Thailand.

A vast majority of Indians are very comfortable with travel by train. With the paradigm shifts in India in the automotive sector, and the investments being made in the roads and the highways sector, more and more Indians are getting used to movement by road in private vehicles. This trend is evident from the quantum jump in road traffic, not only within the cities, but in inter city travel. Disposable incomes are also increasing. As it is, the number of Indians in the middle-income group is in hundreds of millions.

Outbound Tourism

The number of Indian tourists travelling abroad is increasing by leaps and bounds. Many countries are targeting this sector in a focused way. The per capital expenditure of these tourists is also considerable.

In Nepal, for example, the number of Indian tourists has always been very high. While significant numbers of these tourists travel by air, the number of Indians who visit Nepal by road is in lakhs. During important festivals such as Shivratri, there are long queues to enter the Pashupatinath temple in Kathmandu. And one notices droves of Indian buses, which have ferried them from across the border. Similarly, during the festival period of Ram Navami, the area around Janakpur is literally overflowing with Indian tourists.

Similarly, the number of Indian tourists visiting popular destinations in South East Asia, including Thailand, Malaysia and Singapore has been continuously on the rise.

India and Thailand are maritime neighbours as well. There is potential for increasing tourism further, including between destinations such as the Andaman and Nicobar Islands and Thailand, which is not too far away.

The Future of the India-ASEAN Dialogue Through Land Route via Myanmar and Thailand

The road connectivity between India and ASEAN has existed for millennia. This gave rise to rich cultural, trade, academic, and professional exchanges, which have enriched both India and the countries of the region in a very profound and significant manner. As road and rail links continue to improve between India and the ASEAN countries, the people-to-people exchanges would tend to increase proportionately. Historically our bonds have always been very strong. There exists a pan-Asian cultural identity between our various countries. With greater exchanges this would be further strengthened. It would be a voyage of re-discovery for a large number of people in Thailand, in India, and for the people in the other ASEAN countries around Thailand.

The View from Cambodia

The Khmer temples in Thailand, Cambodia, Lao PDR, and the Champa temples in Vietnam, would be a great source of attraction for tourists from India. The numbers of cultural tourists and the "pilgrim" tourists could be very substantial. Similarly, there is a tremendous amount of interest amongst the Buddhists of Cambodia, Lao PDR and Vietnam to visit the Land of the Buddha. The opening up of these rail and land routes, which would pass through Thailand, could, therefore, prove to be very beneficial for Thailand.

Some Suggestions

The proposed establishment of the Thai Cultural Centre is another important step in the further strengthening of the age-old historical bonds between our two countries, and in expanding the depth and content of the cultural relations. In view of the tremendous potential for generating mass-based cultural and pilgrim tourism from India to the countries to the east of Thailand, it may perhaps be useful to consider whether some representation could be given to the great cultural and historical sites located in these countries. It is not difficult to imagine the interest, which could be aroused in the Indian psyche, to visit sites such as the Wat Phu, Angkor Vat and the Champa temples, besides all the interesting sites in Myanmar including Pagan, and in Thailand such as Sukothai and Ayuthaya.

Indo-Thai Relations in the Twentieth Century

GANGANATH JHA

❖

Indo-Thai relations have witnessed upswings as well as downturns in the 20th century. When India was fighting a war against Colonialism, Thailand stood by us. They offered strategic assistance when the INA was established. They provided us a strong base, training grounds and propaganda channels. Thai support for India and the rapport between Netaji Subhas Chandra Bose and Field Marshal Phibun Songgram was totally undiluted.

Thai leadership thought that if India won the war of liberation it would be a victory for all the countries in the region. It would secure "Asia for Asians" and shatter the myth of Western supremacy. The INA could not lead the independence struggle after the death of Netaji, but it shook the foundations of Colonial rule.

India in the post-independence period adopted the path of non-alignment. It wanted to keep Asia away from being embroiled in the Vortex of the Cold War. Thailand on the other hand, felt that communism was a greater threat and containment was the right policy to deal with it. It became a kingpin of the SEATO, and became involved in the Vietnam War. India was naturally unhappy.

India never supported the theory of containment drive and therefore there was rhetoric and polemic but this did not prevent cultural interaction between India and Thailand. Streams of Thai tourists continued to come to Bodh Gaya and look for spiritual salvation in India. They tried to understand the dynamics of mysticism connected with Buddhist Jataka tales or epic heroes Rama, Krishna and Hanuman.

Thus both India and Thailand had a natural tendency to be attracted towards each other. Buddhism was a link and the Thais treated India as a place of pilgrimage. There are several religious practices in Thailand which have a striking resemblance with Indian customs. For instance, the festival of Songkran and Loi Krathong have similarities with the Holi and Chatha festivals respectively. The system of spirit worship and ancestor worship prevalent in Thailand have similarity with Sandhya and Havan in orthodox Brahmin houses.

The cultural links are important but there are geopolitical, economic and strategic links also which govern the relationship and this paper will try to examine these. However, the most important asset in our relationship is religion. The faith in Buddhism is universally adhered to in Thailand and the meaning of Buddhism as defined by Reverend Ashin Thithila is as follows:

> Buddha is one who has attained bodhi; by bodhi is meant wisdom – an ideal state of intellectual and ethical perfection which can be attained by man through purely human means. The term Buddha literally means the enlightened one – a knower – and it is the name of honour bestowed upon the Indian sage Gotama after obtaining enlightenment under the Bodhi tree at Buddhagaya in India. Gotama was born as the son of an Indian king on the border of modern Nepal, about 623 years before Christ. To mark the spot as the birthplace of the greatest teacher of mankind and as a token of his reverence for him, the Emperor Asoka erected in 239 BC a pillar bearing the inscription. Here was the Enlightened One born. Gotama spent his early years in ease, luxury and culture. His father, the King, tried his best not to let him see anything unpleasant and ugly. In his twenty-ninth year, however, when Gotama went to the royal park, he saw on his way an old man, a sick man

> and a dead man, and he realized that all, without exception, were subject to birth, old age and death, and that all worldly pleasures were only a prelude to pain. Comprehending thus the universality of sorrow, he had a strong desire to find a remedy for this universal sickness of humanity.

Buddhism became the religion of various Asian countries before the beginning of the Christian era and India continued to send monks, priests and missionaries to explain the gospel of Buddhism. This was halted only after the Moghuls consolidated their rule in India and tried to propagate Islam in the region.

Historical Background

Indo-Thai relations date back to times immemorial. Thailand is part of Suvarnabhumi, which finds mention even in the Ramayana of Valmiki written in c. 1000 BC. Later, when Buddhism emerged, Suvarnabhumi became well known in India. In 329 BC (Buddhist Era 300) Ashoka the Great deputed Sona and Uttara to Suvarnabhumi to spread the gospel of Buddhism. It is believed that Sona and Uttara went first to a city now called Nakorn Pathom (Nagar Pratham), in Thailand. The residents of Nakorn Pathom welcomed the missionaries and became the first people in Suvarnabhumi to accept the Buddhist religion. Situated at a distance of about 40 kms from Bangkok, Nakorn Pathom is today a place of national importance for the Thais. There is a huge pagoda there to mark the place where Sona and Uttara gave their first discourse on the greatness of Buddhism and laid the foundation for the spread of Buddhism in the rest of South-East Asia.

It is not only from India that Buddhist missionaries went to Thailand. Burma, Ceylon (Sri Lanka), and Indonesia also sent their missionaries in course of time. King Jayanaga of Sri Vijaya (Indonesia) sent a missionary to spread the Mahayana cult of Buddhism in AD 700 (BE 1300). Another important missionary came from King Aniruddha of Pagan (Burma) to spread Hinayana Buddhism in AD 1000 (BE 1600). Most important of all were the missionaries who went there from Sri Lanka in the 13th century. In 1253 some Thai Buddhist monks went to Sri Lanka and returned with the Pali version of the holy Tripitaka. They also asked some monks of Sri Lanka to visit Sukhothai. During the reign of Rama Khamheng of Thailand, some Buddhist monks of Sri Lanka went to Thailand. King Rama Khamheng requested them to settle in his capital, Sukhothai. These monks were experts in the Theravada cult of Buddhism and exercised much influence on the Thais. King Rama Khamheng embraced Theravada Buddhism and made it compulsory for all the future kings of Thailand. He also proclaimed Theravada Buddhism his state religion. Theravada Buddhism continues to be the state religion even today.

The year 1253 is a landmark in the history of Thailand in many ways. It was during that year that the Thais finally defeated the Khmer Government and founded their own kingdom in Sukhothai. In later years King Rama Khamheng (1283-1317) of Thailand developed very cordial relations with the then ruler of China, Kublai Khan, who blessed him to expand his territories at the cost of the Khmer Empire. India was then by no means a powerful country because it was facing repeated invasions on its western frontier. It was under Muslim rule, and Islam had started spreading. Muslim rule was not conducive to the spread of either other Buddhism or Hinduism in the region. On the other hand, the Burmese, the Khmers, and the people of Sri Lanka strongly believed in and practiced Buddhism. The Thais, therefore, looked to them for enriching their treasure of thought and literature regarding Buddhism. Though during the Moghul period and thereafter hundreds of Thai monks continued to visit Sarnath (in Uttar Pradesh) and Buddha Gaya (in Bihar) on pilgrimage, India was in no position to influence the Thais.

Cultural Heritage

For many centuries cultural contacts between India and mainland South-East Asia were disrupted because of external invasion and internecine war amongst the rulers. This did not, however, totally spoil the cultural influence of India already assimilated in those countries. When we observe Thai styles and practices in the fields of religion and philosophy, art and architecture, sculpture and painting, dance and drama, language and literature, we can easily see this striking affinity with India's.

Even today in Thailand both Brahmin and Buddhist rites are observed. The ceremonies at which the Brahmins officiate are the coronation of the King, Piti Raek-Na-Kuan (a ceremony connected with ploughing), the tonsure ceremony, and the swing ceremony.

The Brahmins perform most of the rituals relating to the coronation of the king. They conduct the *homa* ("fire sacrifice"). They also supervise the ceremonial bath, the elaborate preparation of consecrated water, purification, and anointment. Then along with men of the highest rank, they lead the king to the Octagonal Throne. During the actual ceremony of coronation, it is the chief of the Brahmins who hands the Great Crown of Victory and the royal regalia to the king. The chief of the Brahmins also takes precedence over all others in paying homage to the king. The king then receives benediction from the other Brahmins, who are the first to receive his commands. The Buddhist benediction follows later in ceremonies in which the Brahmins take no part.

The second important ceremony in which the Brahmins play an important role is Piti Raek-Na-Kuan. The king chooses the Minister of Agriculture to play the part of Phya Raek Nah ("Lord of the Festival"). The Brahmins give him a choice of three *panungs* ("lower garments"). If he chooses the longest, rain is supposed to be abundant during the year. Phya Raek Nah ploughs a number of furrows and plants rice, which the farmers eagerly gather and plant with their own paddy seeds for good luck. The bulls that pull the plough during the festival are then presented with seven varieties of grain to eat; from the variety they choose, the Brahmins foretell the year's best crop. Piti Raek-Na-Kuan is a national ceremony of Thailand. Both the king and his ministers attend it. It is usually celebrated in the month of May.

The Brahmins play a similarly important role in the tonsure ceremony. This ceremony is a private one for princes between eleven and thirteen years of age.

Lastly, there is the swing ceremony, which is celebrated each year during the second lunar month in the Vishnu Temple opposite Sao Ching-Cha on Dinsaw Road. Before the accession of King Mongkut (1851-68) to the throne, this was also a State ceremony. The Brahmins carry the image of Lord Vishnu and place it on a swing on this occasion. In India, too, the image of Lord Krishna is placed on a swing on the occasion of Janmashtami, the date of His birth. This ceremony is called "Palana" in Delhi and Uttar Pradesh, "Jhula Parva" in Bihar, and "Oonjal" or "Thottil" in Tamil Nadu. This ceremony is still widely celebrated all over India.

Thai architecture as exemplified in the Royal palaces and the Buddhist wats bears a close resemblance to the temples found in India. Archaeologists find in Thai architecture an amalgam of the styles characteristic of the Gupta period (North India) and the Pallava period (South India), as also of the Khmer style (Cambodia) and the style obtaining in Sri Lanka. The Wat Arun in Bangkok has a *trishula* ("trident") at its top as in the temples of Shiva in India. The image of Lord Buddha seated on a lotus in the various temples in Thailand inevitably reminds us Indians of the image of Lord Vishnu or Lord Shiva seated on a lotus in the various temples in India.

Thai paintings derive their themes from the Buddhist Jataka tales and from the episodes in the Ramakien (Ramayana) and the Mahabharata. The Temple of the Emerald Buddha in Bangkok, which is considered to be the most sacred in Thailand, has a series of murals containing the whole story of the Ramayana. To the Thais, Rama is a symbol of goodness, virtue, and piety; Sita, an apotheosis of womanhood; and Hanuman, an embodiment of humour, ingenuity, and gaiety. Evaluating the Indo-Thai cultural links, Prince Prem Purachatra, former Thai Ambassador in India, once said: "The hierarchy of Hindu gods and goddesses provided inspiration to our Thai artists, and some of them have assumed symbolic significance, such as Vishnu, the patron of engineering and science, and Ganesh, the patron of fine arts. We award guilded statues of Saraswati to the winners of Thailand's top cinematic honours."

Thai classical dance and drama – the Khon ("masked play") and Lakorn – derive their themes mainly from the Ramakien and the Mahabharata. The folk dances of Thailand remind us strongly of the Manipuri style of dance in India.

In the field of language and literature, we find that there are many words of Sanskrit and Pali origin in the Thai language. The literature, being essentially religious, is full of mythological tales of Buddhism and Hinduism. Ramakien or Ramakirti is the most exalted of literary works in the Thai language. Though there is a slight difference in the presentation of Thailand's Ramakien and India's Ramayana, yet the basic story is the same. In India, the Hindus attach a religious significance to the Ramayana, but in Thailand, the State religion being Buddhism, such a significance is held by the holy Tripitaka.

Some Thai festivals like Sonkran and Loi Krathong remind us of Holi and Chatha Parva in India. On the occasion of Sonkran, which is celebrated in April every year, all the paraphernalia of Holi are followed. The only difference is that the Thais do not use coloured powder (*avir*), but they use water, mud, dust, and other things. The streets in Thailand are full of jolly boys and girls participating playfully in this festival. On the occasion of Loi Krathong, which is usually celebrated in November, little lamps are set afloat on the water in the canals and rivers with great pomp and show. In India too, on the occasion of Chatha Parva in Bihar and Uttar Pradesh lights are floated on the river Ganga. In Bihar, lights are found afloat even in small ponds. Patna's Chhatt is famous all over India for its illuminations and general participation.

The Thais are very fond of seeing Indian movies, and they import Indian movies on a large scale. They translate the dialogue into the Thai languages before screening them. Indian movies attract huge crowds.

Visit of Rabindranath Tagore to Thailand

Poet Rabindranath Tagore's visit to Thailand in 1927 is a landmark in Indo-Thai relations. Tagore felt very happy to find traces of Indian culture in Thailand, so much so that he wrote:

I come, a pilgrim, at thy gate, O Siam,
to offer my verse to the endless glory of India sheltered
in the home,
away from her own deserted shrine,
to bathe in the living stream that flows in thy heart,
whose water descends from the snowy height of a sacred
time
on which arose, from the deep of my country's being
the Son of Love and Righteousness.

During this visit, the Government of Thailand requested Rabindranath Tagore to send a scholar who could enlighten the Thai people on Indian civilization and literature. On his return to India, Tagore sent Swami Satyanand Puri, previously known as P. K. Sen, to Thailand. Swami Satyanand Puri was thereafter attached to Chulalongkorn University in Bangkok as Professor of Sanskrit. He wrote several books and articles in the Thai language and in English to promote understanding and goodwill between India and Thailand. He had a personal rapport with Premier Phibun and was able to elicit his co-operation in organizing a front to support Indian independence. He was one of those who requested Netaji Subhas Chandra Bose to come to South-East Asia and lead the Indian National Army (INA).

Satyanand Puri also founded an institution called Dharmashrama in Bangkok in 1930. This institution, known as the Thai-Bharat Cultural Lodge since 1940, has played an important role in the life of the Indians in Bangkok. At present the Lodge arranges religious meetings every Sunday. It runs a school where Indian and Thai children study together. The medium of instruction is the Thai language. The Thai-Bharat Cultural Lodge also has a library named after its founder, Satyanand Puri. The literature in the library is about ancient Indian and Thai cultures. Members of its staff help people (especially students) from India visiting Thailand and the Thais visiting India.

When Netaji Subhash Chandra Bose came to South-East Asia in the early forties to lead the struggle for independence, he received invaluable organizational facilities in Thailand. There seemed to be excellent rapport between him and the then Prime Minister of Thailand, Field Marshal Phibun Songgram. Thailand offered not only its land but also its information media to the INA to promote the cause of India's liberation. Thai Government broadcasts gave full publicity to promote the cause of India's liberation. Thai Government broadcasts gave full publicity to the activities of the INA in all the major languages of India. Netaji organized the INA from among the Indians in South-East Asia. At the end of the Second World War, Burma fell once again into the hands of the Allied forces. On the eve of its fall, Netaji shifted the Burmese Office of the INA to Thailand. As the INA was running short of arms and ammunition, he then left for Singapore with a view to proceeding thence to Japan to obtain arms and equipment. However, the plane in which he was travelling crashed under mysterious circumstances, and he died en route to Japan. After his death the INA became defunct. In the same month (August 1945) the Second World War also ended. Thailand began to adjust its foreign relations according to the situation then obtaining in the region. It wanted to show that it had already abandoned its policy of helping the Japanese and sought to cultivate Britain, France, and the other Powers dominant in South-East Asia. INA volunteers were criminals in the eyes of the British Government, and if Thailand had ordered their repatriation at that time, Britain would have been pleased. The Thai Government, however, was kind and sympathetic to the INA. It granted political asylum to almost all the people connected with the INA. This gesture of friendship towards India provided solid ground for friendship between the two countries. India won its independence after two years, in August 1947. It was natural to believe that Thailand's relations with free India would prosper rapidly, but it did not turn out that way in the years following Independence.

Relations after 1947

During 1947-76, neither the King nor the Prime Minister of Thailand ever came to India on a State visit. In 1972, after twenty-five years of independence, President V. V. Giri of India visited Thailand. There were many reasons for the absence of warmth in Indo-Thai relations.

First, there was a difference in the international outlook of the two countries. India became an ardent advocate of non-alignment and peaceful co-existence after getting independence from British rule. On the other hand, Thailand strongly supported US military presence in the region, especially after 1950. It also provided bases and manpower to the United States to put down Communist movements. From 1948 to 1973, Thailand remained under the dictatorship of three military strongmen – Field Marshal Phibun Songgram, Field Marshal Sarit Thanarat, and Field Marshal Thanom Kittikachorn. It became a founder member of the South-East Asia Treaty Organization (SEATO) in 1954. It even allowed Bangkok to be the headquarters of the SEATO. Although the developments in the region and especially in Thailand were not positive for India, yet our diplomats worked hard to cultivate friendship.

India attached geo-strategic importance to Thailand and friendly gestures were shown on the eve of its independence. In February 1947 India's interim government extended a loan to Thailand, which was the first given to a foreign country. The loan was Rupees 50 million to be paid in installments. India on its part, adopted a very sympathetic attitude towards Thailand on the question of payment of reparation, which had been dictated by the British government. The war claims were $5,224,220 to be paid to Great Britain and in which India's share was one-fifth $104,484. On the other hand, Thailand adopted a very sympathetic attitude towards INA volunteers who preferred to stay back in Thailand, and facilitated their rehabilitation.

In December 1946, India appointed a Consul General to Bangkok and B. Dayal was deputed to go there. Thailand reciprocated this gesture by deputing Thanat Khoman to work as the first Charge d'Affairs in New Delhi. Thanat Khoman, who later became the Foreign Minister of Thailand, was succeeded by Luang Pimitaksorn as the first Thai Minister in New Delhi, and B. Dayal became his counterpart in Bangkok. Both governments decided soon to upgrade diplomatic relations to the ambassadorial level in 1951, when Thailand appointed Luang Wichitwadhakarn as the first Ambassador. Though diplomatic interaction was taking place, the regional environment and domestic developments in Thailand were not complimentary to boost Indo-Thai relations.

Thailand in the post-Second World War era, was witnessing civil unrest. Thailand's ethnic Chinese were unhappy because of the communal riots in Bangkok and communist movements were picking up momentum. The communist takeover of power in China and their open support to the Chinese population in Thailand had created a hostile atmosphere. The Chinese had accelerated propaganda drives against the military rule of Field Marshal Phibun Songgram in Thailand. On the other hand, there were disturbances in Patani, and national security was a matter of prime concern for Thai decision makers.

The United States knew the strategic importance of Thailand in the containment drive and they had started showing common concern with Thailand. The US had appointed Edwin F. Stanton as Ambassador to Thailand, who astutely cultivated relations with military elites and thus the two countries came closer to each other. Thailand and the US signed military assistance agreement in 1950 and they founded the SEATO in 1954 and became allies. Thailand became the headquarters of SEATO and thus contributed contingents of armed forces in the Vietnam War. Thailand gave its air and naval bases to the US and the American Airforce regularly used those bases to bomb communist belts in Vietnam. When the war finally came to an end in 1975, Thailand became a frontline state to prevent Vietnam in expanding and consolidating its influence in the region.

However, a number of economic reforms (Doi Moi) in Vietnam since 1986, the signing of the Cambodian peace accord (1991) and the disappearance of the Soviet Union (1991) changed the global security and economic environment. The Uruguay Round of talks, WTO, human rights issues and the rise of radicalism generated new challenges and this diverted the opinion of the countries in the region to attend issues of regional concern.

In retrospect, we find that the cold war of the two super powers had intensified the disputes in the region wherein the ideological and strategic issues predominated the deliberations at the regional and global level. The China factor and Cambodian crisis were the preoccupations of nations in the Asia-Pacific. Although the end of the Cold War in 1991 offered some new opportunities, some new challenges also emerged. Accordingly the countries of the region began to review their old policies and alignments. Indo-Thai relations, which had been marginalized as a consequence of the cold war, got new life and meaningful dimension in the post-cold war era. Both understood the importance of one another and took initiatives to make the relations more vibrant and beneficial. The Indian Premier, Rajiv Gandhi had done some necessary homework when he went to Thailand on an official visit in October 1986. This was surprisingly the first visit by an Indian Premier to Thailand after independence in 1947.

Prime Minister Rajiv Gandhi tried to provide economic dimensions to the existing relations and thus the Indo-Thai Joint Business Committee (JBC) was established to explore possibilities of promoting trade, cultural and educational interaction. This committee suggested some measures to promote bilateral trade and both sides showed keenness to implement it.

The Thai Premier Chatichai Choonhavan later took an initiative to strengthen ties. He reciprocated the visit of the Indian Premier and came on a state visit to India in 1989. Being an astute businessman, he admired the role of the JBC and wished to upgrade it. Hence, the JBC was renamed the Indo-Thai Joint Business Council/ Indo-Thai Joint Trade Commission and entrusted with the task to promote trade on the lines suggested earlier by the JBC. Premier Chatichai took personal interests in the success of the JBC and business targets for 1990-92 were fixed in New Delhi. The bilateral trade picked up momentum, and both sides felt happy at the satisfactory progress.

It is interesting to know that the trade turn-over was quite encouraging. According to the Joint Trade Commission spokesman, the trade plan projected for 1990-92, had been achieved in 1991 itself. The target of US $ 1 billion was achieved within 18 months and there were prospects of boom. India exported gems and precious stones, cotton and fabric, machinery and parts, urea and fertilizers to Thailand, while imported pulses (Moong and Urad), rubber, machinery, synthetic fibres and inorganic chemicals. The export of gems during 1989-91 rose from 10% to 75% and earned India about $ 600 million, cotton and fabric about $ 60 million, and leather and fodder about $ 40 million in 1991. The Joint Trade Commission in the meanwhile explored avenues of trade in other sectors like textiles, machinery, pumps, diesel engines, vehicle parts, organic and inorganic chemicals, dyes and hand tools.

India's investment relations with Thailand also started growing. Being ranked the 13th largest investor in Thailand, India is involved in 20 joint venture projects in the fields of textiles, rayon, chemicals, dyestuffs, iron and steel products. India and Thailand agreed to expand collaboration in fishing, including joint ventures in deep sea fishing, fresh water and brackish water prawn farming, fish processing and study of tuna in the Andaman Sea.

Mr. P. V. Narasimha Rao gave new thrust to India's "Look East" policy and in that endeavour attached great importance to partnership with the ASEAN. He was also interested in improving the investment climate and thought that Thailand could play a key role in that endeavour. He therefore decided to pay a state visit to Thailand coinciding with the meeting of the Indo-Thai Joint Commission in Bangkok in April 1993. He eloquently underlined the significance of a new orientation in India's foreign policy, in which Thailand occupied a key position as close and contiguous maritime neighbour. Thailand was indeed regarded as one of the gateways to expanding trade, investment and tourism ties with the ASEAN. It had been admired as India's major trade partner and Mr. Rao showed his eagerness for further cooperation and collaboration.

The Indo-Thai Joint Commission was scheduled to meet to set up a target for 1993-95 endeavoured to turn Thailand as one of the largest trade partners of India. New areas of cooperation were being explored and suggestions were given. Thailand has already emerged the sixth largest foreign investor in India. In 1993, Thailand had approved investments worth $ 120 million in areas like fisheries, chemicals, air-conditioning systems, hotel and tourism. Thai companies have also signed agreements with Indian companies for joint ventures in the telecom sector.

As Thailand attached importance to growing relations with India, it sent its Foreign Minister, Prasong Soonsiri to India in November 1993. Besides meeting business people, he met Prime Minister Rao as well. He discussed issues of cooperation in the area of nuclear energy, business exchanges, fisheries and agriculture. Thailand also accepted India's offer of technology transfer in areas like fibre optics electronics including computer software and hardware.

Innovative ideas were evolved to boost investment ties and in that endeavour the proposal of a "growth triangle," is quite interesting. In October 1994, Mr. Surin Pitsuwan, the Thai Deputy Foreign Minister, visited India and proposed a "growth triangle" amongst Sri Lanka, Thailand and India for business and trade. Such a tie is expected to augment supply of raw materials, financial goods and high technology. India, however, was not very enthusiastic in its response.

Thailand reinforced its suggestions for this "growth triangle," when Supachai Panitchpakdi, Deputy Prime Minister of Thailand, visited India in January 1995. He discussed thc proposal with Indian businessmen and unfolded the idea in detail at Secretary level talks. This proposal envisions building a four-lane highway between the Andaman Sea and the Gulf of Thailand. The projection is to construct deep sea ports, refineries and industrial ventures alongside the highway.

In fact, India is unable to take a decisive step in the direction of establishing a "growth triangle." When Prasong Soonsiri had met Rao in November 1993, he had himself suggested that India and Thailand should cooperate in business ventures in third world countries, such as Vietnam. This proposal, later known as "Troika," could involve the partnership of India with various partners of the ASEAN and could produce items required outside the region, but this is yet to be taken up seriously.

In fact, India has suggested the "Troika" to Singapore also for a collaborative endeavour and business in Vietnam. Though the Indian proposals have been welcomed they involved India in business ventures in the SAARC region, namely, Sri Lanka, Bangladesh and Nepal.

The "Growth Triangle" or "Troika," are both aimed at a collaboration involving three countries of the region. But the "growth triangle" has assumed some meaning in the ASEAN countries. They have established this at Johore and Bantam and the three countries –

Singapore, Malaysia and Indonesia – have been benefited by such a venture. However, the meaning and scope of the troika is yet to be explored.

Indonesia, the biggest country of the ASEAN, has also expressed its intentions to be a partner in the "growth triangle" in the Andaman regions with India and Thailand. They emphasized the importance of our collaboration through meetings of the India-Indonesia Friendship Association. India is an important dialogue partner of the ASEAN, in which Thailand is a member. The relations with the ASEAN countries are improving and Thailand has facilitated India to play its legitimate role in the region.

In retrospect we find that the two-way trade between India and the ASEAN countries have grown at a fast rate in the post-1991 period. India's exports to ASEAN-9 (excluding Cambodia) had grown from US$ 1.77 billion in 1990 to US$ 4.31 billion in 1996. On the other hand, India's imports from ASEAN-9 had grown from US$ 1.38 billion in 1990 to US$ 3.97 billion in 1996. The two-way trade between India and ASEAN as per Indian official data has grown more rapidly in the period 1993-94 to 1996-97. The relevant trade turnover has more than doubled from just over US$ 2.5 billion in 1993-94 to 1996-97. This reflects 8% of India's global trade in 1996-97 (up from 6% share in 1993-94). Considering this healthy trend, India has set an ambitious target of US$ 15 billion trade with the ASEAN countries for the year 2000-01.

The major exports from India to the ASEAN countries currently comprise agro-based products such as oil meals, edible nuts (ground nuts), sesame seeds, meat and meat products, textiles including cotton yarn, fabrics and readymade garments, drugs and pharmaceuticals, chemicals including inorganic, organic and agro-chemicals; primary and semi-finished iron and steel, machinery (including textile machinery) and transport equipment, and processed minerals. Apart from further expanding India's exports in the above major items of ongoing exports, the following goods and services have tremendous potential to give a further push to India's exports to the ASEAN countries. These include sugar processing machinery, railway rolling stock, electrical equipments and machinery, gem and jewellery, automotive components, and above all information technology including software development consultancy and training in both hardware and software, construction, health and educational services, and processed fruits and vegetables.

Apart from bulk imports of palm oil and other metals, minerals and primary articles, India can profitably expand its imports from the ASEAN countries of electronic items, computer hardware, electrical equipment, and most importantly services for the construction, maintenance and upgrading of ports, airports, telecommunications centres, roads, bridges, and power stations.

Despite the satisfactory incremental growth of India's growth of two-way trade with the ASEAN countries during the post-1991 period, the basic asymmetrical nature of this two-way trade has not yet materially changed. Thus, viewed from the ASEAN perspective, India still accounted for only 1.17% of the ASEAN's worldwide exports in 1996. Similarly, exports from India had amounted to just 1.05% of total imports of ASEAN in 1996. Clearly the ASEAN's trade relations with India are still much below their potential commensurate with their economic strengths (comparative advantage) and considering the areas still untapped.

Dr. Surin Pitsuwan, Foreign Minister, led a delegation including senior officials and representatives from the private sector to visit India during 8-10 July 2000. Members of the private sector accompanying the Thai Foreign Minister were representatives from the Thai Chamber of Commerce, the Thai Bankers Association, Fishery Association, Thai Computer Association and the Thai businessmen of Indian origin. The Thai delegation held talks with Indian leaders such as the President, Prime Minster, Foreign Minister, Agriculture Minister. Foreign Minister Surin also took the opportunity to meet Indian businessmen and delivered an address at the Confederation of Indian Industry.

During his talks with Indian officials, both sides explored the opportunity to increase the amount of two-way trade. At the moment, the average annual trade volume is only US$ 846 million. The Thai side also proposed to the Indian side its plans for enhancing cooperation in the area of fishery, investment, education, information technology, and culture, and will review the progress in cooperation every three years. Thailand expressed its particular interest in investing in Indian infrastructure projects and invited Indian companies in the information technology (IT) and food sectors to invest in Thailand.

The Thai side also proposed to enhance cooperation with India in international and regional organizations such as UN, BIMST-EC, IOR/ARC and ASEAN. And, Thailand being a chairperson of ASEAN Standing Committee, Foreign Minister Surin invited India to increase its participation in the ASEAN, especially in IT, human resources development, Mekong development, and the "Great Wonders of Suwannaphumi" project.

On behalf of the Royal Thai Government, Foreign Minister Surin concluded two agreements with the Indian Government, which were the Agreement on the Promotion and Protection of Investment and the Agreement on Joint Cooperation for the Peaceful Use of Energy.

Members of the private sector accompanying Foreign Minister Surin had an opportunity to meet their Indian counterparts at the Indian Chamber of Commerce and Industry, the Federation of Indian Industry, and importers, to explore business opportunity in areas such as computers, banking and finance, IT, automotive parts, and agro-industry.

Bilateral trade between India and Thailand amounted to US$ 248 million in 1991 rising to US$ 644 in 1995-99 and remained the same in 1996-97. Indian exports to Thailand have gone up steadily in the 1990s, as have Thai exports to India. Exports to Thailand rose 58.6% in 1993, went up by 18% in 1995 and registered a growth of 16.2% in the first half of 1996. Thai exports increased 12.6% in 1993, went up phenomenally by 159% in 1994, rose 49.3% in 1995 but dropped by 16% in the first six months of 1996. The decline was in keeping with the general decline in Thai exports. The major items of Indian exports to Thailand are diamonds and stones, primary and semi-finished steel, plant solvent extracts, chemicals, dyes, raw and finished cotton, drugs and pharmaceuticals and machinery. Thai exports to India have comprised pulses, rubber products, electrical machinery, tools and metal scrap and gems and ores, including rice at certain times.

Investment proposals from Thailand in the fields of fisheries, chemicals, air conditioning systems, hotel and tourism were approved in 1994-95. Indian investment of US$ 25 million in Thailand was registered in the same period. At present there are 27 Indian joint ventures in Thailand involving about US$ 16.5 million. The total approved investment from Thailand for the 1991-98 period was Rs. 24517.21 million.

It is again a reality that India shares the Thai perception about the security vacuum in case of the American withdrawal from Southeast Asia or on potential threat emanating from China, the northern neighbour. They have similar views on the question of sovereignty over the Spratlys or on ethnic conflict or terrorism in the region.

However, Thailand and other ASEAN partners are presently interested in economic relations and in exploring the South Asian market. They may like to expand their economic influence through India in South Asia and treat India as the gateway to enter into the SAARC market.

Thailand is a key regional actor. It has been taking landmark steps in the promotion of business and trade. It endeavoured to turn Indo-China into a marketplace and facilitated the construction of the Lao-Thai friendship bridge. Now it is giving new thrusts to the "Look West" policy and in that connection attaches prime importance to India for its success.

Thailand has evolved a "Look West" policy to compliment India's "Look East" policy. Thailand's Foreign Affairs newsletter stated that the conceptual basis of the "Look West" policy for Thailand is to cope effectively and efficiently with the rapid changes in the international political and economic environment in accordance with the reality of the post cold war era. The "Look West" policy is also derived from the fact that Thailand recognizes the promising economic potential of other regions beyond Southeast Asia. The main objectives of the "Look West" policy as they summed up are as follows:

(i) to strengthen the existing bilateral relations with the target states, and;

(ii) to seek potential markets and investment opportunities overseas and to promote foreign investment in Thailand.

Target states are countries in South Asia, Middle East and Africa. But South Asia is a gateway to the Middle East and Africa. In that connection there is special reference to India, where they find promising economic environment, vast economic potential, cheap labour and abundant natural resources.

In fact, Thailand had taken an initiative in 1995 to establish a sub-regional group involving India for greater cooperation in the name of BISTEC, and this evoked a positive response. On 6 June 1997 this sub-regional grouping was formally launched and the main areas of cooperation included cooperation in trade, investment industry, transportation, infrastructure, science and technology, human resources development, energy fisheries, agriculture, natural resources and tourism.

A special meeting of the BISTEC took place in Bangkok in December 1997 where Myanmar too was admitted to the grouping. Hence BISTEC was renamed as BIMSTEC and decided to establish an Economic Forum with both private and public sector participation from member countries.

Again Economic and Trade Ministers of BIMSTEC met at Bangkok on 7 August 1998 where India was represented by commerce Minister R. K. Hegde. This meeting underlined BIMSTEC's substantive economic agenda and market a significant step towards further institutionalizing BIMSTEC cooperation. A BIMSTEC Senior Economic Officials Committee (SEOC) was established and the responsibilities for the various sectors identified for cooperation were delegated amongst the five countries, as follows:

Bangladesh	Trade and investment
India	Technology
Thailand	Transport and Communication
Myanmar	Energy
Sri Lanka	Tourism and Fisheries

Thus we find that Indo-Thai relations are on the right track. Whether it was economic or security matters, both of them have similar views. They are evolving common stands in the WTO and on free trade. However, it can be found that all these matters are constantly in a flux and depend on existing circumstances. What binds India with Thailand on a permanent basis is Buddhism and, therefore, we must attach importance to cultural contacts.

Contributors

Srisurang Poolthupya is Professor Emeritus and Fellow of the Royal Institute of Thailand.

Chirapat Prapandvidya is Associate Fellow, Royal Institute, Bangkok, and Advisor to the Sanskrit Studies Centre, Silpakorn University, Bangkok.

Sombat Mangmeesukhsiri is Lecturer, the Sanskrit Studies Centre, Silpakorn University, Bangkok.

Amara Srisuchat is Director of Ramkhamhaeng National Museum, the Fine Arts Department, Ministry of Culture, Thailand.

Sone Simatrang is Assistant Professor at the Faculty of Decorative Art, Silpakorn University, Bangkok.

Nophadol Chartprasert is Assistant Professor, Department of History, Faculty of Liberal Arts, Thammasat University.

Sachchidanand Sahai is Professor and Fellow, Indian Institute of Advanced Study, Simla.

Om Prakash is Professor and Fellow, Indian Institute of Advanced Study, Simla.

Satya Vrat Shastri, an eminent Sanskritist, is former Professor and Head, Department of Sanskrit, Delhi University.

Mandavi Singh is Professor and Dean, Faculty of Dance, and Head of the Department of Kathak Dance at the Indira Kala Sangit University, Khairagarh, Chattisgarh.

Pradeep K. Kapur is Joint Secretary (SAARC), Ministry of External Affairs, New Delhi.

Ganganath Jha is Professor, School of International Studies, Jawaharlal Nehru University, New Delhi.

Neeru Misra is Senior Programme Director, Indian Council for Cultural Relations, New Delhi.